V. MCELGUNN

STITCHED AND STUFFED ART

Stitched
and
STUFFED
Art

by Carolyn Vosburg Hall

**contemporary designs
for
quilts, toys, pillows,
soft sculpture
and
wall hangings**

DOUBLEDAY & COMPANY, INC.
Garden City, New York
1974

acknowledgments

Books of this kind are created with the help of many people. I would like to thank all who assisted me to assemble this book in the form of a mini-museum and especially: the artists for contributing their works; Rachel Martens, crafts editor, Farm Journal, Inc., who helped bring the book into being; my family for their encouraging support and particularly my daughter Claudia for her typing; Robert Vigiletti who photographed several works and taught me how to do the rest; Nancy Yaw, Kathy Smith, Leslie Masters, and others.

Library of Congress Cataloging in Publication Data

Hall, Carolyn Vosburg, 1927—
Stitched and Stuffed Art.

1. Quilting. 2. Pillows. 3. Soft toy making. 4. Wall hangings. I. Title.
ISBN 0-385-07188-4
TT835.H33   746
Library of Congress Catalog Card Number 73–20987

First Edition
Book Design by Bente Hamann

Frontis: "Untitled" by ROBERT GOETHALS

contents

STITCHED AND STUFFED ART

ZAP

Claudia Hall

Bright orange, red, and pink shapes make the bursting central form. The background is purple, magenta, and hot-pink synthetic fabric. Filling is a pre-quilted batt of polyester that will not shift inside. Quilting is hand sewn.

soft art from fibers and fabrics... a new/old art form

Art is a form of magic, turning ideas seen only in the mind into real images for others to see and touch. People are awed by this remarkable ability of the artist to create significant forms from paint, clay, metal, or fiber. Many yearn to make things too. Some have discovered to their delight that they do not need to master the complexities of difficult techniques and materials to create "art." A skill as simple as sewing can result in beautiful art works.

This discovery simplified my life several years ago. As an artist I painted, sculptured, and wove pieces to be exhibited in galleries. As a wife I sewed toys and clothes for the children, drapery and bedspreads for the house, and other useful and colorful objects. It seemed to take a surprising length of time to realize that the skill I had learned in sewing could be combined with my knowledge of art techniques to create "soft art."

Soft or stuffed art is a name for the many kinds of art objects that are made from fibers and fabrics. Fibers come in all textures, colors, and sizes from cotton sewing threads and woolly knitting yarns to the more unusual sturdy linen, gossamer silk, shiny plastics, twisted ropes, and a variety of synthetics. Fabrics are formed from this great variety of fibers.

1

A "stuffed art" piece is simply an art object that is stuffed. This definition allows for including a wide assortment from quilts to soft sculpture, from folk to fine art, and from useful articles to eye-pleasing art works.

Stuffed art exists as a category that crosses into several kinds of art. Some people use this means of working to make fabric paintings; others construct soft sculpture and some do functional crafts in fiber and fabric. Stuffed art pieces have a common origin of soft, flexible materials given dimension by some kind of stuffing.

Some stuffed art pieces are primarily useful—such as quilts, pillows, body coverings, toys, and furniture. Some are mainly conceptual art works that are used to delight your eye and beguile your mind. These include wall hangings, soft sculpture, environmental pieces, and experimental pieces that are hard to categorize. The choice of work selected for this book is based largely on finding good ideas well presented in this field.

Making soft or stuffed art allows for the pleasure of working in nearly all the ways of artists: with color and design, texture and line, or three dimensional form. It also makes use of the homey arts of hand and machine sewing for quilting, appliqué, embroidering, smocking, patching, and stuffing or other familiar techniques to give form to fabrics.

Fortunately, nearly anyone can sew. This useful skill is not limited to women. Many of the world's best tailors, fashion designers and "soft artists" are men. Children, too, can manage simple sewing to make useful objects. Our young son sewed small cotton sand bags on the sewing machine to use in re-creating historic battle scenes for his toy soldiers. Sewing is a most handy skill.

Modern life gives us an easy familiarity with fibers and fabrics since they are such an integral part of living. Look around you to see how common these soft materials are in your surroundings. Most likely your clothes are of fabric and also, perhaps, the seat of your chair. Sheer-fabric curtains may soften the light from the windows and a nubby rug may cushion your feet. Terry-cloth towels dry you and canvas tents shelter you from the weather. It is difficult to imagine life without fabrics since they are so much a part of the way we live.

From direct experience we know how fabrics drape and fold, how they stretch and hold. We know how they feel and what they can do, whether to keep us warm, dry, sheltered, or to make us appealing. Creating with fibers and fabrics means that we can usually begin with a ready understanding of the materials.

Materials and tools for sewing are easier to obtain than many other art supplies. Stores everywhere carry needles, thread, and all kinds of fabrics.

Left-over scraps or worn-out clothing, collected ribbons or feathers, old buttons, empty cloth bags, and other discards can provide free materials to make a layered, quilted, or stuffed art object. Stitching can be done with a ten-cent needle or an expensive sewing machine; either makes equally fine seams.

Another appealing feature of this kind of art is that it's relatively easy and adaptable. Materials are usually lightweight and flexible. They can be gotten out and put away and aren't messy to work with. It's possible to pick the size of project to fit available time, space, and energies. Sewing manages to fit into a busy household, limited space, or short bits of working time more easily than most creative projects.

The primary reason for choosing this type of art is the nature of the materials. People choose art forms that are created with materials they respond to most. Sculptors seem to like to struggle with hard stone and metal. Painters like the easy fluidity of paint. Many people respond to the color, texture, and feel of textiles. It is so easy to be intrigued by the characteristics of fibers and fabrics and the way they can be formed into endless imaginative shapes and designs.

Soft art objects have a special beguiling quality. The remembered familiarity of the materials suggests a ready friendliness with the piece. Taking advantage of this nostalgia, a friend who was moving to another state collected her scraps and mine to make friendship quilts for each of us. I designed and she sewed. And I still can't help recalling: Here is my daughter's dress, my friend Pat's sofa cover, her son's shirt, and our bedroom curtains. People commonly identify with their clothes and possessions in this manner. Soft sculpture takes advantage of this association. Its strongest appeal comes from the way the maker has combined familiar elements into a new form which is still soft, well sewn, and nostalgic, but different and unique.

Soft and stuffed art is now tremendously popular in many forms from folk art to fine art. It has always been enjoyed as a way to make useful and attractive home objects. Many of these made by imaginative craftspeople have found their way into bazaars, boutiques, and art shows. More recently many professional artists have been creating fabric forms, often called "fabrications," that are shown in important museums and galleries. The Museum of Modern Art and the Museum of Contemporary Crafts, both in New York, have presented shows including this medium.

Perhaps this emphasis on soft arts as one of the most outstanding ideas in contemporary art reveals a warm and wonderful trend to honoring individual handcraft skills again after a highly industrialized era. It could also be considered a healthy return to respect for all abilities; not book learning or physical skills alone, but a combination of knowing and doing. I am delighted to find an art form that includes folk and fine art, useful and non-functional art works, and serious or fun pieces all in one way of working.

The only limit to making stuffed art is what you can think up and then figure out how to execute. Reproducing other people's art works may be quite instructive, but creating your own is soul satisfying. With so many other people experimenting with this art, you can use their concepts as well as your own ideas to plan projects. Books and magazines provide information. Working with friends, seeing art shows, and thinking in terms of soft and stuffed art helps to decide what to make. Each piece you make has a way of suggesting others as you work through the problems to the finished object.

This points up the greatest value of all in making stuffed art—the chance for personal expression. I can think of few greater joys than creating a work of art that turns out as I had planned and yet reveals unexpected touches that just grew naturally in the making. Each piece I make teaches me something about creating or about the nature of materials or something about myself or the way of the world. This pleasure in making a piece of art is strong in everyone, from the child running home waving his first drawing to show the family, to the famous artist contributing expression of basic truths. The joy of creating is for everyone.

and so this book...

Based on my own work in this field and occasional stuffed art pieces that I came across in my tour of galleries as art critic, I knew that a ground swell of stuffed art was underway across the nation. Collecting examples of stuffed art objects from people everywhere became a treasure hunt since this art in its current form is fairly new. To help in the search, I asked our community art center, the Bloomfield Art Association, for permission to put on a "Quilts, Coverlets, Soft Art Objects" exhibition.

People from all across the country submitted 150 entries by photograph. Two outstanding people in this field agreed to serve as jurors to select the works for the show—Gerhardt Knodel, who is head of the Department of Textiles at Cranbrook Academy of Art, and Nancy Yaw, who is co-owner of the James Yaw Gallery. Only forty pieces were selected for the show by the jury, due to space limitation and personal choice. More of the original 150 entries are shown in this book.

Large crowds came to see the show when it was hung at the Bloomfield Art Association. Viewers' responses revealed a lively interest in this kind of art. There was no tiptoe-reverently-through-the-hushed-gallery with this show. Visitors voiced opinions immediately, they touched the pieces, checked the back side for construction secrets, tried on the soft jewelry, and verbally rejuried the show to their satisfaction. "I like this wall hanging better than the prize winner." "What is a bag of stuffed groceries doing in a quilt show?" "Does a traditional quilt belong in a stuffed art show?"

Most people who see a show like this do not separate the idea from the object and how it is presented. They either like it or they don't. This is natural. The artist's aim is to mold the idea, the materials, and the technique of construction into a complete whole. Of course this doesn't always happen. Some uninspired ideas are beautifully made and some innovative ideas are not very well presented. It becomes quite easy to find good ideas if you are involved with making things yourself, because you are looking for them.

Other exhibitions described in later chapters contributed art works for this book. They too were good "idea" shows. Some work included in this book will look strange to the novice eye. And some will seem elementary to the professional artist's eye. This mixture is intentional. One of the most stimulating trends in recent years has been the blurring of strict category lines. Painters are working three dimensionally. Sculptors may paint their works. Weaving is no longer necessarily flat. The era of mixed media or combinations of materials is here.

As early as the 1950s "big name" artists began working with materials and fabrics in other than traditional ways. Stitchery artists have been working with them all along but began to handle them more like painting and sculpture. With both craftspeople and fine artists working with the same materials, the final artificial separation of fine arts and crafts has diminished.

Certainly some of this attitude still remains. Perhaps you have heard friends say, "I need some art for my house. Guess I'll get a painting." It usually does not occur to them that a wall hanging is essentially the same thing—a significant image on fabric. Once people have made this discovery, they can choose art to make or to have that uses materials they respond to most.

Painters might argue that their work is more intellectual. Nevertheless, the current trend shows more respect for soft materials and the touch of the

AMERICAN SYMBOLS

Carolyn Hall

Both the revival of patriotism and the current rebellion against the Establishment have made the flag a popular subject. It has been sewn on jeans and jackets, made into sleeping bags and clothing. Curiously, it has been used both to show honor and respect as well as anger and disregard.

The 39×60″ flag is assembled from lightweight fabrics: cottons, rayon, silk, synthetics, and laces, many of which have a printed or woven design. The colors remain red, white, and blue with variation from blue-reds to orange-reds and turquoise-blues to navy blues. Seams are machine stitched, top is quilted by hand.

6

artist's hand. These materials can be and are used by people everywhere to make useful objects and fine art pieces as well. Anybody might come up with a good idea.

More appreciation of the intuitive style of the folk artist has developed. Folk art and fine art influence each other, resulting in the mixed bag of today's lively expanded art world.

This does not mean that no standard of value exists in judging contemporary art. An agitated woman student called me, as critic for a newspaper, to ask, "Are there any rules now in art? My instructor says there are but that they can be broken. What kind of rules are those?"

Her instructor probably means to say that over the years guidelines have developed. "Art works should have balance." "Colors should harmonize." Rules like these developed because most good art works possess these characteristics. But balance and harmony are variable qualities. For instance, two equal-sized children can balance on a seesaw, but it takes two tons of ants to balance an elephant. That's a much more exciting scene to imagine. Either choice of stable or precarious balance is available for designing art works. And for people who like to stretch the rules, there is a way to make one ant balance an elephant.

Rules of art are generated by the art work itself. If you are making a classical painting, the finished work should meet the standards of classical paintings. If you decide to make a quilt, it should be well made and imaginatively designed. It is beside the point whether a classical painting or a quilt is better. Each piece must meet its own standards.

Some of the pieces we include in this book are very simple, showing a nice little idea well done. Others are complex in construction and concept. They are bigger ideas well done. All are presented as a survey of what is going on in stuffed art in a variety of forms. The collection begins with quilts, the flattest of the stuffed art forms, which contributed sewing techniques to this movement. Soft sculpture is presented—it's the new-idea field. The chapters that follow—featuring toys and furniture, pillows, and wall hangings—show the many ways in which these techniques and ideas are used. The last chapter presents experimental and environmental works.

PATCHWORK QUILT

Ursula Reeves

1. contemporary quilts

Grandmother's quilts have been discovered again. Antique buffs have always valued patchwork quilts as story books of the past. Currently everyone seems to enjoy them as a homey art form. People are making modern patchwork quilts in a variety of new forms, new colors, and new materials.

I was delighted to find an old family patchwork quilt several years ago, though I didn't realize at the time that other artists were also rediscovering our American heritage in the form of quilts, handmade antiques, primitive wood carvings, and other folk art forms. Prevailing ideas and attitudes seem to float in the air for everyone to share.

Quilts were strictly utilitarian items in the beginning, made as warm covers for beds and as hangings to cover ill-fitting windows and doors to keep out the cold. Patchwork itself grew out of a need for economy— using left-over pieces of fabric.

In an earlier revival in 1933, Carrie Hall lauded quilts in her book *The Romance of the Patchwork Quilt in America* as ". . . a homecraft art that has played no small part in the growth and development of American life . . . from the earliest Colonial times to the present day. First as a nec-

9

essary part of pioneer homemaking, then as a product of an awakening desire for beauty in the home, and now this twentieth-century revival is an appreciation of that art, which of all the time-honored household arts has withstood the machine age and by no means reached its climax." Carrie Hall's prophetic words herald a new era in quilt making.

What's different about the current respect and affection for this folk art form is that serious artists as well as homemakers are interested. Sources for art forms can arise from any part of society. Artists of the 1920s and 30s imported their main influences from abroad, as from the French modern painters, or glorified the workers and the common man here at home, as in the American "ash can" school of art and the Mexican murals on social revolution.

Historians of the future may be able to pinpoint why this happy meeting of folk art and fine art is occurring now. Perhaps they will discover that abstract and conceptual art became too esoteric, too related to itself for any but the most devoted art lovers to understand. Or they may discover the opposite, that conceptual art has led us out of a specialized art world of strict categories in painting and sculpture into a wider appreciation of the world around us that includes our past and present love of handcrafts.

The contemporary quilts collected for this book reveal a respect and nostalgia for the traditional construction and character of the old quilts. Some people made quilts closely resembling the older prototypes. Some used newer design shapes and colors and yet still sewed the quilt in traditional ways. In later chapters, people use the typical quilt-making techniques to construct totally new objects that have little resemblance to quilts. Generally, the traditional quilt form serves as a painter's canvas on which to work out designs expressing ideas.

quilting materials

Two ancient kinds of needlework of widely different character are combined in quilts. Patchwork is the art of piecing together fabrics of various kinds and colors. Quilting is the method of fastening together with stitches layers of cloth to secure firmly the "filling" or padding enclosed. Both methods of sewing were brought from Europe with the earliest settlers.

Quilts keep people warm. The layering of fabrics, whether cotton, wool, or others, entraps air to hold in body heat and keep out cold air. Stitching the several layers together means longer wear, too.

The stuffing or padding layer can be thick or thin depending on the desired warmth or the design idea of the quilt. Thin paddings such as sheets or old woven blankets need fewer quilting stitches to hold them in place. Loose fibers such as cotton, wool, polyester fiberfill, shredded foam rubber, and down or feathers make puffier quilts.

Quilts include three kinds of construction. The pieced quilt combines pieces seamed together in various ways. Usually these traditional patterns developed long ago were geometric and worked in portable-sized squares. Patterns were characteristic of various pioneer groups, the theological New Englanders, the home-loving Dutch of New York and Pennsylvania, and the luxury-loving Virginians. Traveling west after the Revolution, pioneer women delighted in exchanging patterns and inventing new ones. Most early quilts before 1776 were pieced.

The second form of patchwork quilt is the appliquéd—"laid-on"—or patched quilt. This was considered more elegant than the pieced variety but, surprisingly, the homey crazy quilt uses the laid-on technique. Appliqué became popular just after the Revolution and reached a peak of popularity about a hundred years later. This kind of quilt may require more working space if the pieces that make up the design are laid on full-sized backing fabric.

The third kind of quilt is the quilted counterpane. The surface design results from padded or corded quilting. Called trapunto, this kind of work is often augmented with additional padding stuffed into different parts of the design during construction. The quilting stitches created a puffiness. This puffiness can be modeled like a bas-relief sculpture to make raised designs.

In addition to these traditional quilting techniques, the quilts included in this book also show several ways of coloring the fabric: dyeing, painting, and screen printing.

Newly developed dyes for the individual craftsperson accomplish more professional results. These dyes are fiber-reactive dyes that penetrate the fiber to become part of it. The process is chemical and using these dyes seems fairly complicated in the beginning. Household dyes are easier to use, although sometimes not as bright in color. Tie dyeing is done with these. Household and fiber-reactive dyes are usually used hot, at a ratio of at least 30 to 1 (water to dye stuff). Both can be used cold for painting and printing if the dye is more concentrated.

Some of these techniques are explained more fully in chapters that follow—with illustrated examples that show specific results.

ANTIQUE QUILT (ABOUT 100 YEARS OLD)

Owned by author

"Crazy Quilt" is the traditional name for this style of random designed laid-on patchwork quilt, done by an anonymous Hall ancestor.

FARM SCENE (opposite page)

Carolyn Hall

The road to Grandmother's house across the Mid-Western countryside, past textured squares of earthy-colored fields, inspired this family patchwork quilt. The design was adapted from sketches eight-year-old Garrett Hall made enroute. Oriental perspective, so natural for children, stacks the scene vertically with important objects enlarged. Size: 4×7'.

PATCHWORK STITCHERY DETAIL

Pat St. Cyr

This stitchery evokes the mood of traditional patchwork quilts and demonstrates both the piecing and appliqué techniques.

"Piecing" is the name given to the traditional method of sewing patterns of fabric pieces together to form the quilt face. Usually these designs were elaborate geometric patterns worked out by the quilter, or passed along from one to another until they became traditional patterns with familiar names.

By appliquéing squares on squares and letting her pieced squares ramble casually in uneven rows, Pat St. Cyr conveys the charm of an earlier era. The pleasure of this quilt lies in the lively colors and the contrasting variety of fabrics from a plush velvet to a sturdy twill.

In the old days, the exquisite and complex geometry of the quilts highlighted the handcrafted look of their surroundings. Today, craftspeople strive to give a softening irregularity to our highly technical society. Most contemporary quilters design their own patterns and work in a loose, less-controlled manner.

PATCHWORK QUILT (entire piece on page 8)

Ursula Reeves

Brilliantly colored, richly textured knitted velour, and satin provide material for this 63×87"quilt. Ursula Reeves selected available colors in velour, then dyed, tie dyed, and bleached some of the pieces to get a rich range of colors before starting the quilt. Each square is framed with a zigzag of colorful embroidery.

AMY'S QUILT

Jo Ewald

Jo Ewald stumbled onto the joys of quilting by searching for a way to keep her hands busy and her mind stimulated. The idea of the quilt for her daughter came from one of the many craft books she researched for a suitable activity. Other books, magazines, friends, and neighbors contributed ideas and drawings for the squares picturing things and activities Amy liked.

She learned new skills as the quilt grew in size. Vaguely remembered childhood embroidery stitches were recalled by taking a stitchery class. Local quilters showed her how to assemble the finished work by placing the assembled blocks over a layer of polyester fiberfill padding and permanent-press sheet backing. The layers were basted together and fixed in sections to a lap frame for quilting. The pattern of quilting stitches follows the squares.

Completed size of the quilt measures 72×96". The background is white with an assortment of colors, patterns, and weaves used in the figures.

The designer's lack of trained drawing skill gives this piece a modern folk art appearance. An innate, lively sense of design and a consistent simple style of presentation results in a totally delightful quilt. Mrs. Ewald views herself modestly as a Michigan housewife and mother. She says, "The whole experience of turning out something that people admired was so heady that I was encouraged to go on from there." And she has.

PASTORAL QUILT

Gina Gustafson

This design is quite spontaneous and was not mulled over. "I just cut out shapes, often suggested by the scraps themselves, and sewed them down by machine," says the designer.

"I started in the center with the house. Then I sewed the cutout shapes onto the big fiberfilled square, four or five pieces at a time, working gradually out to the edges. I used double-knit scraps—they do not have to be hemmed since the edges will not fray.

"For me, the quilt design combines humor and fantasy. There is a cow at a stop sign, a horse in a pagoda, the purple mountain's majesty, and other funny little subjects to look for. The quilt depicts a fantasy-type land of trees, brooks, animals, a little house, and elements of a story book. It was fun to make and now it's fun to have."

The quilt is approximately 60″ square and is done in fanciful colors.

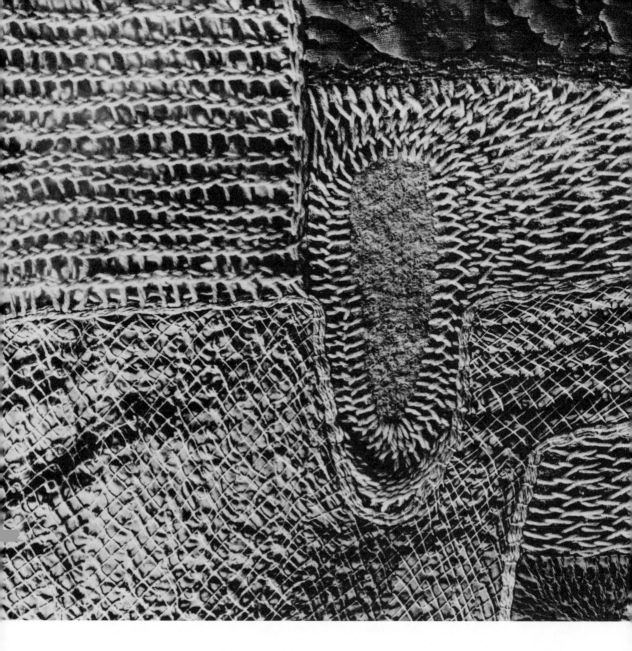

BATHSHEBA'S BEDSPREAD

Alma Lesch

Allover embroidery provides a lively way to create surface texture, pattern, and color. Embroidery is also one of the main traditional techniques for embellishing fabrics, joining seams, appliquéing, and quilting. Stitches fall into three types: straight stitches, loop stitches, and knot stitches.

Completely covered with complex rich textures and colors, the quilt measures 78×106". It was included in "Objects USA", the major Johnson's Wax exhibition which traveled the United States and Europe.

QUILTED TRIANGLES

Bonnie Johanna Gisel

This artist experiments with the quilt format by purposely exposing the seamed side. Wool triangles are hand stitched onto larger muslin triangles. These are machine stitched together to make squares. The artist enjoys breaking up shapes and putting them back together, playing a mathematical game by manipulating the forms.

"I wired the squares together so that there was some breathing space between squares," the designer explains. "If I had stitched them together, it would have been too tight and impossible to read the individual squares and the lines around each."

The intentionally rough 5×6′ piece is dyed with muted natural colors of blues and browns, and still harbors a few burrs from the field.

BABY BLANKET

Diana Gordon

Painted ceilings of the Renaissance era, that show a view of heaven as you look up, surely influenced the design of this baby comforter. You see the underside of a white bird as it flies beneath white puffy clouds and a yellow sun with ribbon rays against a little blue cotton/polyester sky. Surrounding this celestial scene is an atypical navy blue background which provides a deep blue night for the yellow appliquéd and quilting-stitched stars. The clouds are softly stuffed with polyester and gathered slightly at the edges to allow extra fabric for the puffiness. The entire quilt is hand sewn, including the ribbon edging. It measures about 3×4'.

TIE DYE QUILT

Gwendolyn Hogue

The artist selected a delicate silk for her quilt top—an ideal fabric choice for the subtle range of colors achieved with tie dye.

Colors of this piece range from black and shades of gray to touches of golden dawn. The finished dyed silk is quilted to a burlap backing through a layer of polyester padding. Size is 36×60".

ERMINE THROW

Carolyn Hall

To create the appearance of fur by the use of the tie dye technique, I began with white cotton suede cloth, (called "gray goods" by the commercial fabric printers). First I dampened the piece. The large 4×7′ size required that I work on a Ping-Pong table where the piece was folded in long accordion pleats. String tied tightly around the folds at 6-inch intervals gave an orderly pattern. The bundle fitted tightly into an electric roaster containing a gray, hot household dye bath. The strings and the lack of movement in the dye bath prevented the dye from penetrating much of the fabric, resulting in the linear patterns shown.

The softly dyed gray-and-white suede cloth is machine stitched along fold lines to polyester padding, backed by dark gray wool. Tweedy gray-and-white tassels complete the piece. The quilt has had extensive use as a coverlet for naps and as a sleeping bag for children.

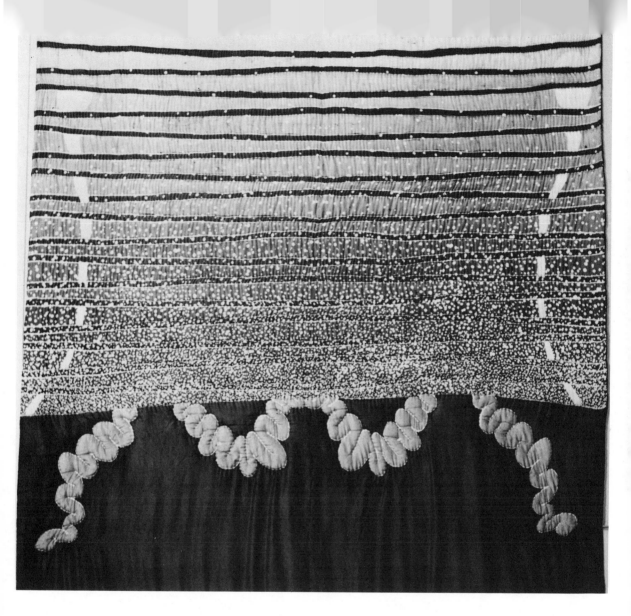

BATIK QUILT

Philip Warner

This graduate student is noted for his sensitive batik drawings on wall hangings. About this quilt Philip Warner says, "It was my aim to create a functional quilt as important, aesthetically, as the wall batiks I make. It was important to use the voluptuousness of quilting to add to the depth of the piece."

Colors in this quilt range from a dark maroon to soft tans, greens, and the original white of the silk. Polyester filling and a velvet backing complete this striking 8×10' quilt.

NUMBER 1

Ron King

Color is so important to most artists that sometimes they purposely de-emphasize it to re-establish contact with texture and form, as in this example. Silver Mylar, white wool fabric and black fur give richness to this 7×7′ quilt.

The silver tubes are made individually from oblong sections of Mylar gathered at the ends. The tubes are sewn together, stuffed and then sewn to the backing. Several different weaves of white wool are used for the patchwork background.

SCREEN PRINT QUILT

Marlene Cox

This artist uses the quilting technique in combination with screen-printed fabric for rich effect. Screen printing is a stencil process which allows for a more elaborate design than an open stencil. A film of lacquer or glue or other opaque resist material is adhered to a fine-mesh screen fabric which has been stretched tautly on a frame. Dye stuff is mixed with thickeners to make a paste which is pulled across the screen with a squeegee. The dye prints through the fine mesh where there is no resist. Each different color usually needs a different screen. The reusable screens can make small and detailed or large designs. Fiber-reactive dyes are used since they penetrate to become part of the fabric through chemical action. When colors are firmly set with sun or heat and thoroughly washed, they have the feel or "hand" of commercial fabrics. These dyes are a vast improvement over early "hobby" screen-printing paints which left a stiff and imper-manent layer of paint.

In this quilt, machine and hand stitching follow Marlene Cox's screen-printed design. Subtle muted colors in the tan and brown range allow the texture to be foremost.

WEDDING QUILT

James Gilbert

Photography catches the magical reality of the moment. To keep this special quality, this stuffed quilt was printed by the photo-screen process.

Preliminary darkroom work prepared the series of wedding pictures for making a screen. Since the screen prints only solid color, there is no way to get photographic toning or gray shadings. The picture to be made into a stencil must be reduced to black and white. James Gilbert has used several graphics processes to do this: A halftone screen on the photo changes the grays to different-sized dots. (A look through a magnifying glass at photographs in the newspaper will show these dots which simulate shading.)

In another photograph he "dropped out" gray values by excessive contrast. A third more complicated device is "solarizing" the print or flashing it with light to reverse development before "dropping it out." The photo without grays can then be exposed onto a light-sensitive stencil. This is developed and adhered to the screen, which results in a screen for printing.

Photos are screened in red and yellow and arranged serially, as in a movie, on a white fabric to create this life-raft-shaped "Wedding Quilt" which measures about 36×72".

COMPOSITION IN BLACK AND BROWN

Audrey Daniels

Trapunto is a form of quilting in which additional padding is stuffed into selected areas for increased dimension. Most often this padding is added during construction and forced in with long tools—a pencil, scissors, the wood end of an artist's paint brush, or any other handy device.

This small subtle quilt, measuring 3×3′, is stitched along the lines of the screen-printed design. It is fully padded in the brown sections, flat in the black. The velvet fabric both traps and reflects the light and gives additional richness. The quilt received an honorable mention award in the "Quilts, Coverlets, Soft Art Objects" exhibition.

PEOPLE QUILT

Audrey Daniels

Velvet nap, earthy browns and blacks, and full trapunto create a blanket inviting to the touch. The quilt is shown folded to bring out these qualities. Simplified people-shapes provide a central theme, one that the artist has used extensively in other stuffed wall hangings. This small piece is about 36″ square.

IF HER HEART DOES ACHE

Mary Jane Mazuchowski

A brown wool figure on a colorfully striped satin background portrays a person seeking privacy and solace on her bed. Her mental and physical anguish is somewhat lightened by the almost humorous distortion of the figure.

Various sections of the quilt have extra stuffing—the row of pillows, the figure, and some of the satin stripes—to give a sculptured relief effect. This quilt measures 42×70″ and is entirely machine sewn in straight and zigzag stitches.

FLOATING SQUARES

Mary Jane Mazuchowski

"This is one of a series of bed pieces I've designed that show people in a reclining position. The idea of this hanging quilt is to capture the movement of pattern as it moves over and under the figure. It shows how you become part of the bed; when you are lying on it, you blend into it."

The background fabric is calico, commercially printed in reds, pinks, and browns. The figures are dark red; the wandering squares are tan, gold, beige, and related colors. This quilt measures 42×70".

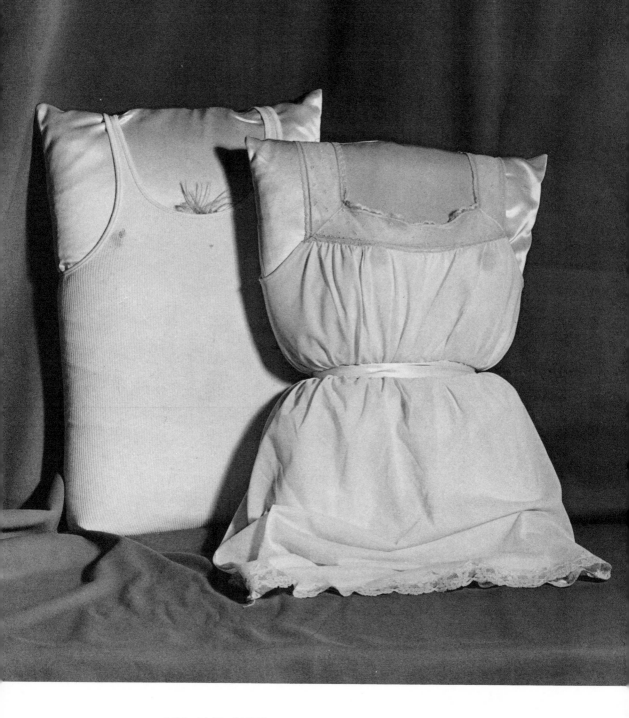

HIS AND HERS

Jan DeVore

Ready-made clothing on pink satin bed pillows economically creates this couple.

2. pillows

Pillow: Anything used to support the head of a person when reposing; especially, a sack or a case filled with feathers, down, or some soft material.

This defines a pillow in terms of function, but more is involved. Anything so common and useful in people's lives as a pillow will be embellished and constructed in a multitude of individual ways. People find reason and need to make them large or small, decorative or plain, and in a variety of colors, textures, designs, or shapes.

Images and attitudes have grown up around pillows because they are so intimately bound up with sleeping. Many children become strongly attached to them as security objects. One of our children loved a hand-woven blanket until it was worn to the warp threads. She hid the bedraggled blanket during the day so no one would comment on its sad state. I made a pillow shaped like a bear's head, with a drawstring at the bottom, to hold the blanket. Then Claudia could see and touch her old blanket whenever she wished. In a few years this plush bear pillow was worn to the threads, too, so I made a larger bear to encase the whole thing. This one outlasted her need.

People commonly invest their possessions with mystical significance for good reasons. With this in mind, the James Yaw Gallery in Birmingham, Michigan, assembled a show called "Pillow as Concept" to explore artists' ideas about pillows. The results were delightful, funny, serious, beautiful, and weird. Examples from this show are included here.

The pillow makes an ideal stuffed art project. Pillows are usually small and simple in shape, and yet offer endless variety in color, form, and materials. Many people who dread the time-consuming magnitude of a quilt can easily make a pillow in as short or long a time as they wish.

The making of a pillow, or any kind of stuffed art, always involves design. Design is the language of art, just as words are the language of thoughts. This formal design vocabulary was developed to describe what artists have learned about creating art. Working intuitively and intellectually, artists learned to arrange component parts of an art work so that the viewers' eyes are led to see relationships, images, direction, balance, rhythm, harmony, or whatever was intended.

The natural order of the world, based on structure of materials, growth patterns, physical laws, and emotional needs, gives the artist logical patterns and guidelines for designs.

So many activities, from creating the most lofty sculptures and paintings, operas, books, or plays to the simpler accomplishments of planting a garden, making a cake, or selecting what to wear, share in common the elements of design. People possess and use these concepts instinctively. In the visual arts the following are among the most important considerations.

COLOR is emotion. It lifts the spirits, calms the soul, delights the eye, and engages the intellect. Color is important to people in practical ways—to tell when strawberries are ripe, to see if you are sunburned, to indicate what objects are made of, to create moods in rooms, to identify traffic lights or fire trucks.

FORM is the space an object fills, real or implied. Form is the line of a drawing, the shape of a sculpture, the dimension of a weaving. Everything has color and form, even a black-and-white photograph that represents a colored pillow.

TEXTURE implies more than soft and furry. It means whatever surface quality exists or even is represented, as in paintings of objects. Texture can be soft, hard, flat, rough, smooth, shiny, grained, papery. Texture is the look and feel of an object, a most satisfying element in design since it appeals to touch as well as sight.

BALANCE is as necessary in art as it is in life. People expect things to behave by the natural law of gravity. Artists use different types of balance for various effects. Art works designed with similar sides, symmetrically balanced have a solid base. Many rows of small woven fibers asymmetrically balanced by one large row of big unspun loops make a less predictable, livelier design.

REPETITION and VARIATION serve the artist in making rhythmic designs. Lines and shapes repeated over and over, as in a woven pillow, create a melodic background like the repeated notes of a song. Varying the repeat produces interest.

EMPHASIS develops by contrast, repetition, size, arrangement, and other means of bringing attention to a special point.

MOVEMENT comes from patterns within the design that generate visual activity and cause your eyes to travel around the piece to see what happens.

HARMONY is achieved by consistencies—of materials, of colors, of forms, of textures—so that nothing jars the senses or disconcerts the eye.

EXCITEMENT comes from vitality of color and texture, from unpredictability in arrangement, from unusual choices of materials, from precarious balance that appears to defy gravity. Excitement comes from the way you feel about the art you create.

RITUAL OBJECT

Jeanne Boardman Knorr

Jeanne Knorr uses traditional materials, leatherlike fabric and feathers attached to cords by wrapping, to project an Indianlike imagery. The piece is not a copy of a historic object but her own selection of form to project her personal feelings. Size is 6×8×14″.

PILLOW

Urban Jupena

The delightful pattern of guinea fowl feathers inspired the related tweed pattern of weaving. The wools of the pillow echo the brown, white, and black colors of the bird's feathers. The 15"-high pillow is shaped like a bag, the elementary shape of pillows. The appeal of rich textures in natural colors is the artist's uncomplicated message in this pillow (left).

FEATHER PILLOW

Carolyn Hall

This pillow was made for the "Pillow as Concept" show which motivated the participating artists to think about the nature of pillows. It harks back to one of the basic definitions: A pillow is a bag stuffed with feathers. The idea is reversed here with the feathers on the outside, polyester stuffing inside. The chicken feathers are dyed bright orange; crocheted tassel is light yellow. The pillow is about 12" in diameter (right).

41

TYPEWRITER

Carolyn Hall

Representation in art is achieved by simulation of the original. Here patterns of keys are transformed into buttons and the case shape is simplified in a soft green velvet with the key mechanism shown by embroidered lines.

This is one of the many examples of simultaneous invention that continually occur. This pillow was made several years ago at the same time Claes Oldenburg made his famous giant-sized typewriter. His is message sculpture with its sagging shape that questions reality. This smaller one, measuring 18×18×5", is a pillow to prop your head on when you've been typing too long.

CAT PILLOW

Carolyn Hall

Animals, domestic and wild, are handsome examples of adaptive design, each singularly styled for the kind of life it lives. I particularly like the way cats move. Perhaps if people were covered with fur, we would appear as supple as they.

This velvet pillow tries to catch the easy dignity of cats expressed by the solid right angle lines of the form. Catlike colors of the velvet upholstery fabric used are warm cream and gold with a faint green-gold cast. Cotton stuffing, a firmer substance than polyester, holds the form upright. The cat is 12×15".

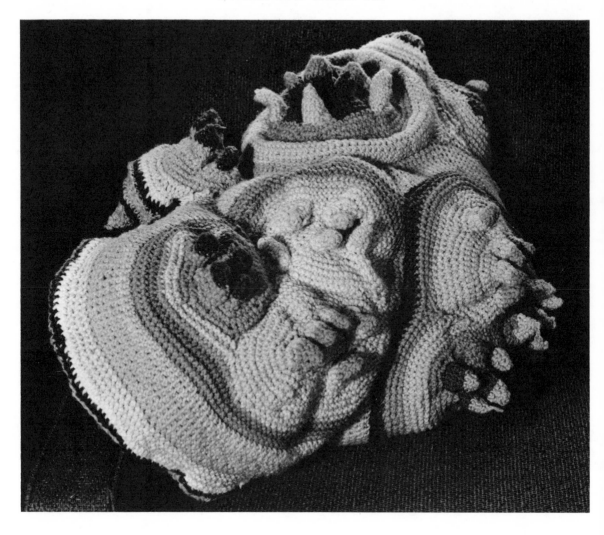

EVERYTHING YOU ALWAYS WANTED TO KNOW

Claudia Hall

Techniques for making fabrics from fibers often suggest forms. Crocheting, like typing, proceeds most easily in a line. Making a circle of the line means you need not turn a corner at the end but can continue to build along the same working line.

In this sculptured pillow shape, Claudia selected colors that are as animated as the design: red, orange, purple, hot pinks, and chrome-yellows. Clusters of finger shapes surrounded by rings grew to mountains and plains. These same shapes were repeated with variation over the entire piece, no two clusters being quite the same in shape and color. The amorphous shape measures about 20×30×12″ and changes whenever it is moved.

44

CERAMIC PILLOW

Ann Kingsbury

Excitement in art often comes through unpredictability. Who would have thought of a ceramic and leather pillow? Functional ceramic pillows have existed in Japan to keep elaborate hair dressings neat, but the use in this pillow is to different ends.

This artist's work always reveals a mysterious spirit. Her works give form to dreams, instinctual urges, and fearsome imaginings. Of course, this makes her pieces controversial because they uncover that which most of us try to keep buried.

Projecting these honest feelings into art gives the work the breath of life. Well-designed pieces can be decorative and attractive, but it is the reality of the artist's individual vision that gives them vitality.

The ceramic disks have pierced holes around the edges through which leather thongs are crocheted in a double row. These pieces are joined by heavy fibered yarns into a pillow shape which measures about 18×24".

45

SATIN STITCH PILLOWS

Helen Bitar

Color commonly ranks as the number one element in a design. As handsome as these pillows are in black and white, they are electric in their rich and ebullient range of color (see color section). Whether the wild and wonderful colors Helen Bitar chooses affect her designs, or whether her design sense insists that she use these colors, cannot be decided. Each goes hand in hand to make her work instantly recognizable.

The pillows are solidly embroidered in a simple satin stitch, which gives texture and dimension to the complex design. Helen Bitar is nationally known; her stitchery is shown in many fine galleries. This pillow is part of the "Objects USA" exhibition. The larger pillow is 20×21"; the smaller, 11×15". See color page 90.

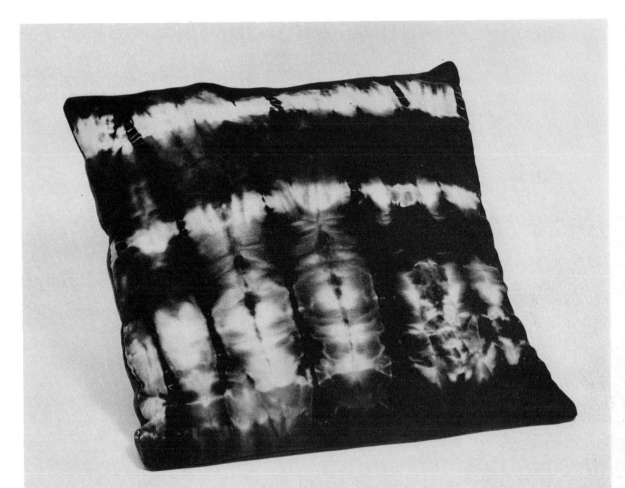

TIE DYE PILLOW

Carolyn Hall

Simple techniques can produce most appealing results, especially when emphasis is placed on the special qualities of the technique. Tie dye produces a characteristic random-shaded pattern that would take hours to duplicate by brush. This 18×18″ square of cotton suede cloth was accordion folded and tied with string at intervals. The cloth was tightly bound at the top which produced a more solid row; loosely tied at the bottom to emphasize the fold. The color is a dark blue with lighter shadings. The velvet back is purple.

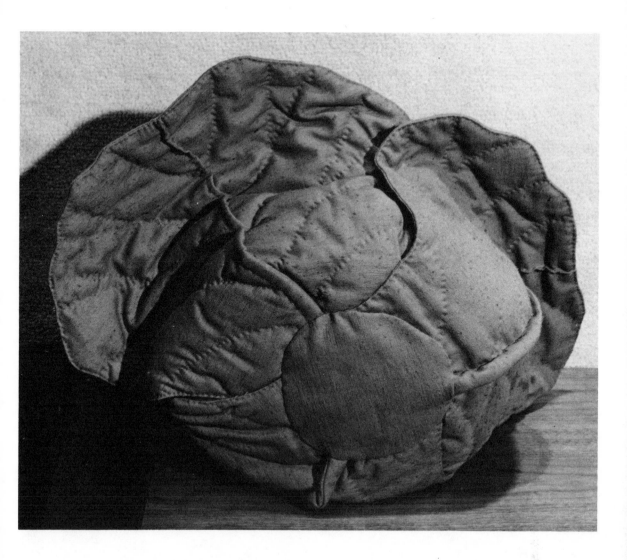

CABBAGE PILLOW

Jean Gillies

Nature provides a wealth of beautiful design patterns and systems for artists to enjoy, to use, and learn from. Natural growth-order inherently possesses harmony and balance, repetition and variation, rhythm and emphasis. The cabbage gives the artist a progression of similar round-leaf shapes, in softly changing shades of green, that form a solid center core. Jean Gillies has translated these leafy shapes in consistent fabrics. She outlines the supporting vein structure with tiny quilting stitches and trapunto folds on the back.

Re-creating a perishable vegetable in more stable materials allows the artist to enjoy both the original and her interpretation of it more fully. The cabbage pillow is life size. See color page 92.

49

PILLOW PEOPLE

Pat St. Cyr

Castles, kings, princesses, and knights catch the fancy of many a modern daydreamer. Illuminated manuscripts and embroidered tapestries remain to tell of this romantic era. The image of these earlier times reappears in contemporary stylized form in these small pillows. Lines, colors, and shapes combine to represent people in a simplified way. We know these are pillows of felt and floss, but we accept them as human forms.

Embroidery to create color and line on background fabrics has been popular since the ancient Orientals perfected this technique more than two thousand years ago.

The sewn line closely resembles the drawn line, a versatile means of delineating small detail or creating large textured areas. The doll-sized pillows range from 8″ to 16″ high.

KNOT PILLOW

Carolyn Hall

One of the delights of working with fibers and fabrics is their flexibility. Materials are soft and yet strong, which allows for shaping and bending them to all manner of forms. Two long tubes of velvet that are about 6″ in diameter and 75″ long can be shaped in a wide variety of ways from single spirals, curves, and knots to double combinations. Colors are analogous browns from tan and cream through rust to black.

53

PORTRAIT PILLOW

Jo Snyder

The grizzled face of the artist's sculptor-husband inspired this portrait pillow. It's made of sturdy upholstery plastic with fabric backing; facial features (also plastic) are machine appliquéd with zigzag stitching. The face is white with tan shading, blue eyes, and black hair. The pillow is softly stuffed with polyester and is 18″ across.

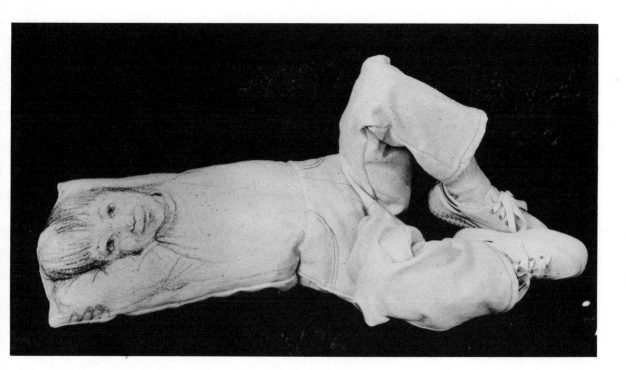

GARE

Carolyn Hall

Part pillow and part soft sculpture, this portrait of Garrett Hall captures the character of a small boy who is a combination of lovable softness and gangly, restless legs. The pillow-shaped top is stuffed with springy polyester filling. Face and arms are drawn on the front and back of the flecked natural cotton/polyester fabric with a grease pencil. Fixative sprayed over this keeps the pencil lines from smudging. The same fabric sewn into jeans and legs with added cotton stockings and tennis shoes completes the life-sized figure.

STAR, CLOUD, AND RAINBOW

Jo Snyder

   Pillows provide one more opportunity for dispersing art works about the home.

   Phenomena of the heavens are the subject in this cluster which shows a silver plastic star, a white plastic cloud with a yellow sun peeking out and a five-tone rainbow in spectrum colors. The pillows range from 1' to 3' in length and are stuffed with polyester fiberfill.

56

MAN CHAIR

Brooke Greeson

Whether this soft giant is pillow, toy, or furniture doesn't affect his humor and charm. The piece appeared in the "Weird and Wonderful" exhibition at the Bloomfield Art Association, a show that emphasized the trend to fetishism and mysticism in art.

Artists, writers, movie makers, and others in the arts delve eagerly into mysticism, the occult, primitive religions, Oriental philosophies and their rediscovered fields of knowledge for ideas to interpret in art. The mysterious aura of this ballooned buffoon is probably unintentional. His fabric body is unbleached muslin. Stuffing is economically furnished by used plastic cleaner's bags.

58

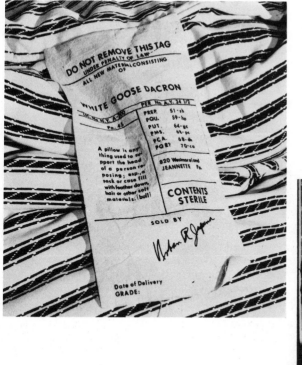

PILLOW AS CONCEPT

Urban Jupena

Scale furnished strength for Pop Art and other contemporary art movements. A familiar object that is much larger or smaller than expected forces increased awareness of its qualities. Certainly the space traveler's distant view of earth and the electron microscope's fantastically enlarged view of matter have vastly expanded our perception of scale. These macroscopic and microscopic views of the world are used to great effect by artists.

While a student, Urban Jupena reproduced his dorm bed pillow to an enormous scale, humorously paraphrasing the warning "Do Not Remove Under Penalty of Law" label. His super pillow measures about 4×6' and is 18" thick.

59

THE WOVEN DINNER

Michael Miller

This wool, double weave life-sized collection of food allows for rearrangement, since the artist feels that people should be able to touch fiber forms as part of appreciation. All pieces are white, with a few green touches.

3. soft sculpture

Soft sculpture is a way of making sculpture from soft materials. Soft sculpture and quilting have qualities in common. Both are rooted deeply in everyday life, both are made from soft materials using sewing and other fiber-forming techniques, and both often deal with nostalgic subject matter. They also differ many ways. Quilting developed as a functional craft—it becomes art only in the hands of an imaginative quilter-designer. This form beguiles with its homey familiarity. Soft sculpture is intentionally non-functional art that employs the appeal of fiber and fabric and yet often tries to shock by the surprise use of incongruous materials.

Soft sculpture appeared on the scene more than a decade ago along with the advent of Pop Art. Claes Oldenburg stands out as the foremost inventor of this art form. This was an idea whose time had come, and soft art emerged from many places across the country at the same time. Oldenburg presented the familiar hard objects, a typewriter or a sink, sewn in softly stuffed oilcloth. They looked like surrealistic or Freudian dream fantasies come true.

This questioning of realities is part of soft sculpture and its close relative, Pop Art. In both, the viewer is urged to take a closer look at life around him. These artists recognized that people tend to keep "art" and "life" separate. And yet they know that whatever people live with influences their lives and becomes a part of them as the cultural heritage of the future.

Some Pop Art implies that everyday life is gaudy and uninspired. Soft art is rarely this harsh, perhaps because it is soft. It often endears the familiar. People like what they know. Where Pop Art intends to mock the commonplace, soft sculpture fantasizes it. The result is often humorous.

A warm friendly humor, the funny look of the incongruous, is common in stuffed art. Humor has never been continuously popular in the fine arts since it is often aggressively cruel in pointing out human frailties. People usually prefer to have their moments of nobility documented in art. Soft art refuses to take life this seriously, portraying familiar objects in a soft-edged form reminiscent of stuffed toys.

The aura of prevailing times is reflected in the art work of an era. It is difficult to sort out directly which attitude of society is pictured in what way, however. The emphasis on the value of the ordinary human being which inspired the rise of the non-hero in stories, and the fear that the "system" dehumanizes us all may both have contributed to this softened, more homey art form.

The main quality of stuffed art, if there can be one with so many artists working in this field, is a celebration of life. Joy and love are the most profound human feelings expressed in art.

Don't worry if you don't have these feelings while you create soft art works. People work intuitively, trusting their own reasons for making things. It is the critic's and the historian's role to explain influences and concepts, yours to make what you wish.

materials

The trend to mixed media allowed soft sculpture to be considered seriously as an art form. Soft sculpture is a means of stating the traditional ideas of sculpture in a new medium.

The materials most commonly used to make soft art are fibers and fabrics, leather, plastics, and other added bits and pieces. The advantages of these include flexibility, variety in texture and color, availability, ease of working, and special character of the materials.

A basic knowledge of sewing by hand and machine is necessary for making stuffed art. Knowing how to draft a pattern is useful, too, although this can be learned by trial and error or careful measuring and figuring.

To construct a three-dimensional shape can present a challenge if the form is to stand by itself. A wire, metal, or wooden support inside can hold the shape upright just as human bones give structure to bodies. The piece can be held aloft by wires from above, or it may be allowed to take its own loose shape. Dorothy Lipski, a graduate student, mentions working at length to construct wooden and wire armature for pieces, finally realizing that for her they looked best when allowed to flop naturally.

Stuffing soft sculptures firmly can hold them upright. The kind of stuffing used and the way a piece is stuffed influences the character of the soft sculpture. The most commonly used stuffings are quilting batts of cotton, wool, or polyester fiberfill. Less expensive stuffings include shredded foam rubber, kapok, wadded newspapers, shredded paper, plastic pellets, excelsior (wood shavings), and plastic cleaner's bags. Unusual stuffings for special effects include dried peas or beans, nylon stockings, boxes, sand, or shotgun pellets. Practically anything can be used if it produces the desired effect.

Some people treat the surface of soft sculpture as hard sculpture and color it with paint or dyes. Others handle it as soft fabric and embellish it with embroidery, trimmings, and sewn-on items.

Sculptures can be formed by pattern sewing of fabrics, or molded by weaving, crocheting, knotting, or basketry. As often as not, the artist selects a mixture of techniques and materials to carry out his ideas.

Many people whose works are included in this book mention that they formerly worked in other media but now work in several ways. Perhaps you will recognize the touch of the ceramist, the painter, the weaver, or the sculptor in these pieces.

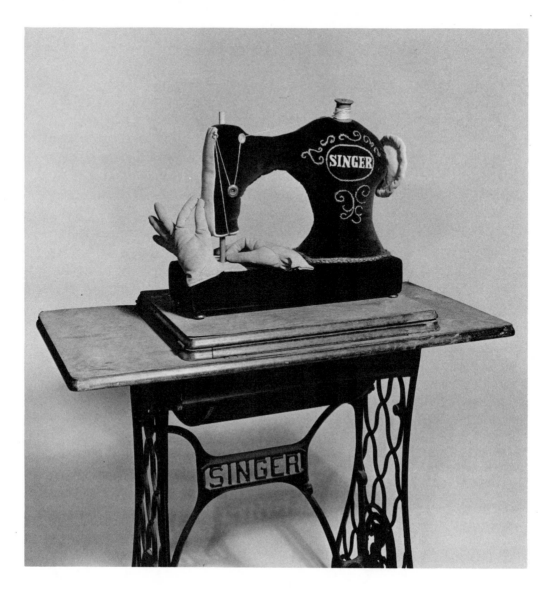

SOFT SEWING MACHINE

Carolyn Hall

This life-sized soft stuffed sewing machine was to memorialize my old machine for the miles of seams it had sewn. Working in a spate of enthusiasm, I cut, sewed, and stuffed a piece of used green velvet into a machine shape, added an empty spool, two dowel sticks, a pair of ready-made gloves, and other bits and pieces. Viewing the completed work gave me a surprise. I hadn't reproduced a likeness of my old machine—I had gone back even further to my mother's older machine on which I had learned to sew! This insight taught me to trust subconscious intuitive ideas, not insisting on knowing exactly why I make something a certain way but waiting to see what I really wanted to say.

64

STUFFED AUTOMOBILE

Carolyn Hall

Art work is often literary in concept, based on the meaning of words. The word "stuffing" brought to mind the usual condition of our station wagon over the years as it was filled and emptied of our children, their friends, our friends, groceries, art works, lumber, dogs, clothes from the cleaners, and an endless list of transportable objects. This car unzips at the back. Inside, two seats full of people and other miscellany hold the roof up. The car is made from satin lining in gold, with silver Mylar trim. Foam lining helps maintain the shape. The inside is lined with a patterned velvet. The car is 27" long, 15" wide, and 10" high.

BIRTHDAY CAKE

Carolyn Hall

This crocheted birthday cake is supersized, 18" in diameter and 7" high, emphasizing the nostalgia of birthday cakes. In retrospect, people tend to embroider a fantasy scene. They make things better, brighter, and bigger than real. The direct pink, yellow, and blue colored yarns describe the sticky sweet frosting so typical of birthday cakes. The cake is balanced on a pedestal cake plate made from a lathe-turned wooden post with a molded door decoration.

Two round foam rubber pillow cushions inside are covered with pink taffeta which enlivens the pink and white crocheted frosting. The new owner of the cake says it is an ideal dieter's cake.

HAMBURGER

Claudia Hall

As a student at Haystack-Hinckley summer art school, Claudia crocheted this life-sized plate of favorites with traditional cotton crocheting string. The circular patterns of crochet are well suited to these shapes. The textured stitch is especially effective in simulating the hamburger meat and crinkly potato chips. Green pickle disks, white onion circles, red tomato slices, and the white paper plate on red-and-black fabric complete the luncheon scene.

LETTUCE SANDWICH

Carlos Cobos

Stuffed green plush lettuce and velvet bread make a whimsical sandwich. Some fabric objects can become soiled by dust in the air or careless handling. Some stuffed art is washable and some is intentionally expendable, based on the idea of use-and-enjoy, then on to the new. This artist encases his 15" soft art in durable heavy clear plastic—makes it easy to keep clean, compact to transport.

DDT

Randall Schade

The common grocery bag stands immortalized with all it implies. This particular piece stems from a reaction to additives, pesticides, and fertilizers. It is the artist's social comment. He sewed and stuffed the food, cutting random patterns from unbleached muslin. The lack of color conveys his message about bleached-out food values. The clear plastic bag, measuring 15×9×18″ high, allows an X-ray view. In spite of its ominous message, the delightful grocery bag exudes a lively humor.

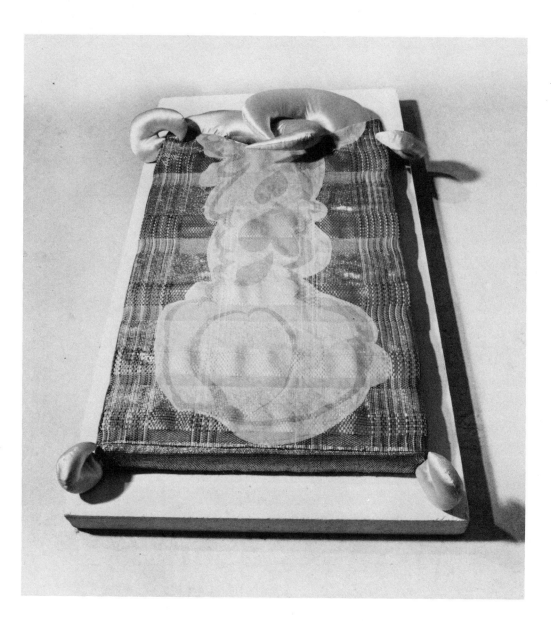

PRAYER RUG

Judith Mills

    An idea based on a specific culture, as the Near East in this one, allows the artist to rely on the rich collection of significant forms, typical colors, and specific ideology that are valued by that group. The stuffed curled "sultan's slipper" shape in peach-pink satin brings to mind a multitude of Persian objects: a scimitar, a quarter moon, a mosque, and others. The woven area mixes varying widths of gold Mylar threads. Perhaps the screen-printed design on a sheer overlay fabric is a genie's smoke. The rug measures about 3×6'.

BOTTLES

Ann Wilson

For this artist, bottle shapes serve as form for contrast and interplay of the floral-patterned printed textile designs. Muted colors absorb and reflect light in their flat and shiny surfaces. They are small pieces, only 9" high, but as fine in their own way as porcelain ceramics. No other message demands your attention, just the pleasure of the shapes and the handsome related surface treatment.

PARADE LADY

Lenore Davis

Decorative embellishments give a festive air to a stately velveteen lady. Gay colors are dye painted, then highlighted with embroidery on the kapok-stuffed 21″ figure. Lenore Davis' figures are closely related to ceramic sculpture.

BLOND LADY WITH INFANT

Lenore Davis

Simplified human forms, in the hands of this skilled artist, express ideas as well as shapes. In design, the baby is part of the mother's arm. This design is more than chance—it shows that the child and mother are inseparable, interdependent.

The velveteen figure has a dye-painted surface, is stuffed with kapok, and is 20" high. The bottom is weighted to keep the piece upright.

Lenore Davis formerly worked in ceramics, but marriage and a move took her away from her ceramics equipment. She turned to soft forms for expression. "It has been a process of translating ideas into the medium, rejecting the many that were better off being made in plastic, metal, or clay."

THE MOUNTAIN WITH CLIMBERS

Lenore Davis

A scroll of shaped stuffed fabric nearly 7' long coils into a spiral to symbolize the circuitous path the climber followed to plant his flag triumphantly on the summit. To emphasize his accomplishment, he is shown in exaggerated proportion.

Dye in a thickened paste allows the artist to paint her shaped velvet forms with all of the nuances of watercolor paintings.

FAMILY REUNION

Lenore Davis

The group, related in personal ways or activities, is welded into a single art object. Individual identity gives way to membership in the group. This idea is expressed in a straightforward way, if not openly humorously, but still ranks as philosophic insight into group dynamics.

Of her experimentation with this means of expression, Lenore Davis says, "Gradually more methods of presenting certain ideas were found—ways of uniting elements such as elementary individual parts to be attached, cutting the entire piece in one if possible. It was always within the technical framework of having to sew the shape and to be able to turn it to its right side."

Only the faces receive special sewn detailing; the rest of the reunion group is cut in one piece and delineated with sketchy dye painting.

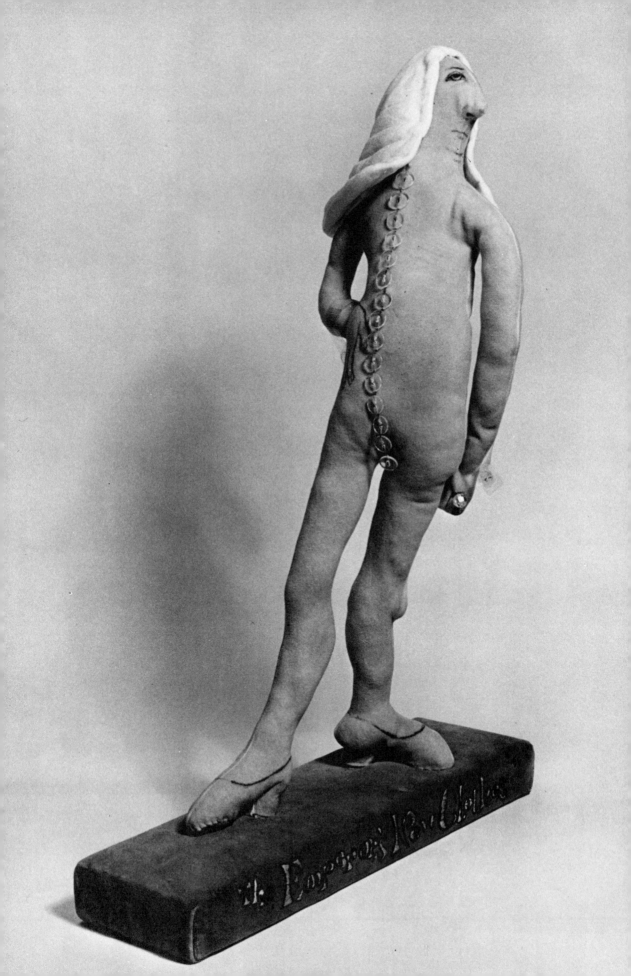

THE EMPEROR'S NEW CLOTHES

Carolyn Hall

Fairy tale people, who reveal our own vices, virtues, and victories, are a delight to portray. This is a fairy tale illustration of the vain emperor who was deceived by clever tricksters into believing that he wore a magical cloth that only the pure could see.

His body is cut from two pieces of white cotton suede cloth—front and back are identical. After the figure was stitched, I dyed it with household dyes mixed to achieve a flesh tone. I drew his face and other details with a permanent felt pen. Clear plastic buttons and details imply his clothing.

"Emperor," designed for a show featuring transparent art works, is based on the rationale that nothing is more transparent than something that isn't there. He measures 22" high.

GROWING SCENE

Claudia Hall

Landscape is sometimes heroic in scale, sometimes tiny. Moss greens, deep rich browns and golds describe the fertile earth with tendrils probing forth, a scene bursting with energy. This small plot of ground, measuring 6×6×9″ high, is of crocheted wool yarns.

BUILDINGS

Susan Aaron Taylor

Flexible forms that can be rearranged at will express this artist's feelings about the cityscape. The row of buildings is triple woven and stuffed during the weaving to achieve dimension and stiffness to support the forms. Hinges are made by a crossover in the triple weave. Natural sisal and wools are used to construct the 16″ by more than 90″ piece.

THE GAS MASK MAN

Michael Miller

Although this artist insists that he made this piece only because someone gave him the gas mask, viewers read into it a protest against polluted air. By use of the gas mask he wittingly or not picks up all of the related horror of war and impure air.

The mechanical complexity of the mask contrasts sharply with the soft woven vulnerability of the figure. A mixture of fibers is used in dark colors. Soft parts are woven on a floor loom, then shaped with stitching. The figure is life size.

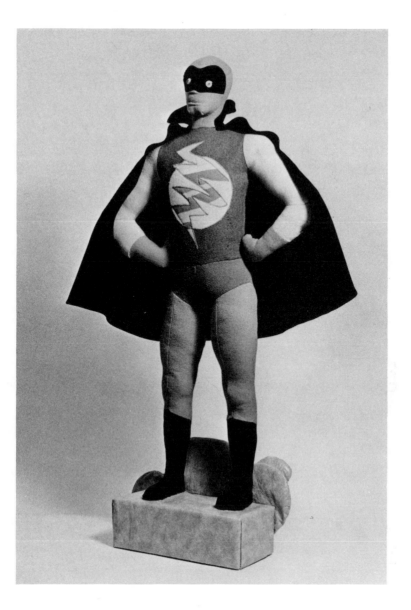

SUPER STUFF

Carolyn Hall

Comic book characters epitomize the supermale, "able to leap tall buildings in a single bound." Round button eyes on this 30" hero-type give him a baffled what-am-I-supposed-to-do-now look that must confront anybody trying to play a superhuman role.

Bulging muscles are achieved by pattern cutting the soft stretchy wool and polyester fabrics to shape. The figure is then stuffed with polyester fiberfill pushed firmly in place. Two dowel sticks running from base to head hold him upright. Colors are all strong aggressive hues of red, orange, blue, magenta, and black.

81

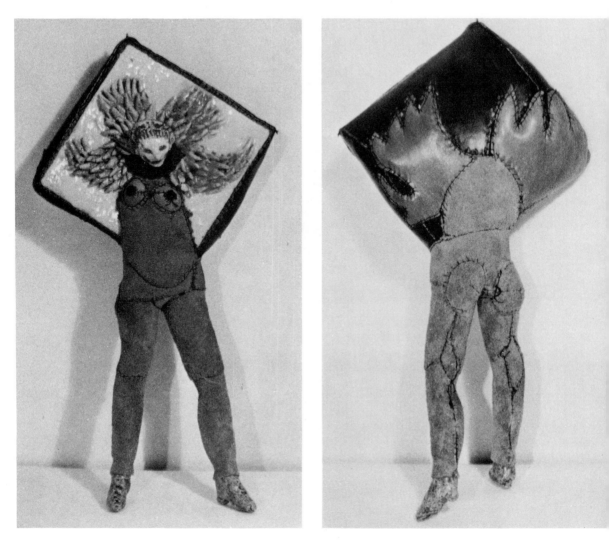

MYSTICAL FIGURE

Ann Kingsbury

Suede and ceramic combine to create this strange mythical female. Hand-stitched lines are used to outline shapes within the overall shape to remarkable advantage. Ceramic feet and head structure glow with colorful low-fire glazes. The earthy texture of the ceramics coupled with the shiny and sueded-leather give a special tactile quality to this small 8″ figure. She is most appealing to hold in your hand.

Ann Kingsbury commonly projects the mystical and macabre with her provocative pieces—beguiling people with their strangeness.

DAMSEL

Bonnie Meltzer

Woman "in all her infinite variety" tempts many to portray her. For this artist she is a fluffy creature dressed in a glittery dress. Her soft floppy shape follows a random exaggerated outline. Bonnie Meltzer's works are not easily explained as she follows her intuition in designing her unusual creations.

Soft fabrics make ideal materials for experimentation with human shapes since the finished figure is often flexible and can be arranged in many ways. Familiar gestures and poses give the viewer a means of identifying types of people. Artists know this and use this in their works, just as people know it and develop individual ways of moving to project who they are. The 54″ figure is stuffed with polyester.

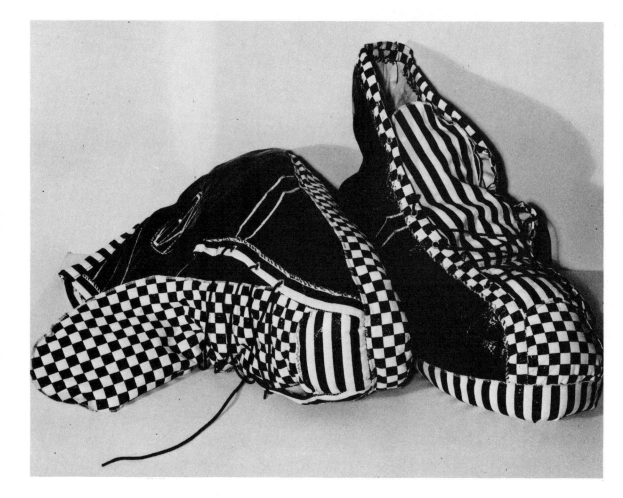

CHECKERED GYM SHOES

Shirley Givens

The gym shoe as a motif in art has enjoyed enormous popularity. People from diverse places commonly work with similar ideas in similar ways. Few are consciously copying others, but all are working from the general intellectual and aesthetic currents in the air. Other series of similar works also appear throughout the book to emphasize this point.

This delightful pair of Keds measures 24″ long and 18″ high. They are shaped in a playful way that invests the shoes with personality. Leather-textured plastic material in black, white, and black-and-white checks form the shoes. Stuffing is concealed within the plastic layers.

MERCURY ADIDAS

Carolyn Hall

Silver Mylar plastic provides experimental material for constructing this giant shoe which is three times normal size. Mythology up-dated evokes images of a modern Mercury dashing about carrying his messages from other Olympic gods wearing the latest in silver Adidas tennis shoes.

The wings are of machine-quilted gold satin fabric stuffed with polyester. Exposed stuffing in the shoe gives the appearance of clouds.

Mylar plastic sews fairly easily on the sewing machine. I laid thin paper under the plastic to allow it to slide easily during the stitching. Metal washers serve as grommets for the shoe laces. Five strands of heavy gray wool are braided (or finger woven) to form a shoe lace which is consistent in scale with the rest of the shoe.

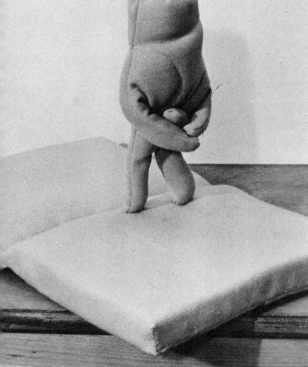

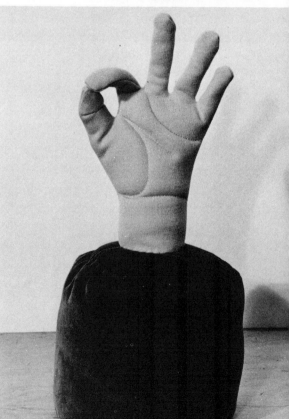

"I HAVE A TRAINED FLEA IN MY HAND"

Carolyn Hall

Hand gestures are so universal in meaning that they have become a language of symbols. The closed hand can refer to the jokes about supposed unique creatures hidden in the hand. Others in this "hand" series are: "Here's the church and here's the steeple," Nixon's victory salute, the A-OK gesture, and "Let your fingers do the walking through the Yellow Pages." The hand is of tan knit fabric on a velvet base embellished with gold fringe. The hands are life size and stuffed with polyester and cotton.

87

SUPER GLOVE

Carolyn Hall

Hands are tremendously important, so things that cover hands become important too. A pair of fur-lined gloves given to me by my husband became my favorites. I like the ease of sliding into them and the way the leather remembers the shape of my hands after I remove them. Since I'm a hopeless glove loser, I re-created one glove in an unlosable 48" size.

Fabrics in the right texture and color are not as easy to buy as colors of paint. I often pick up appealing pieces of fabric when I find them. The simulated brown leather-suede cloth was a remnant discovered on my rounds of the fabric stores. I had admired the cream-colored fake-fur acrylic lining for some time. Stitching on the super glove seams, as with the smaller model, is done by hand to catch accurately the character of the original.

One of Eight Balls, Haruno Iwashiro

TV Dance Special, Lenore Davis

Satin Stitch Pillow, Helen Bitar

Sweet Pea, Daisy Pachl

All Saints Textile Mural, Janet Kuemmerlein

The Liberty Rag Store, Marilyn Poppas

91

Landscape Quilt, Kathryn McCardle

Cabbage Pillow, Jean Gillies

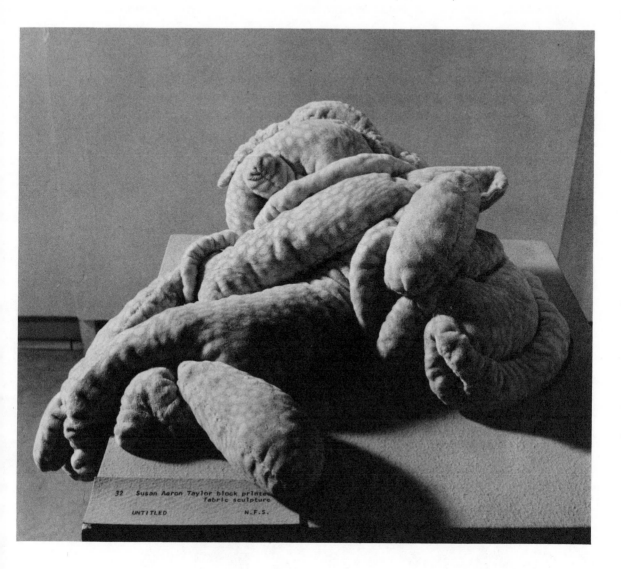

32 Susan Aaron Taylor block printed
fabric sculpture

UNTITLED   N.F.S.

UNTITLED

Susan Aaron Taylor

Abstract shapes free the artist from the need to represent accurately, and allow for experimentation. Shapes and the way they fall due to their weight interest the artist. This small sculpture which is about 12" long is stuffed and weighted with dried beans. The stuffing changes the surface texture of the screen-printed velvet. The shifting weight of the beans causes the piece to lie heavily.

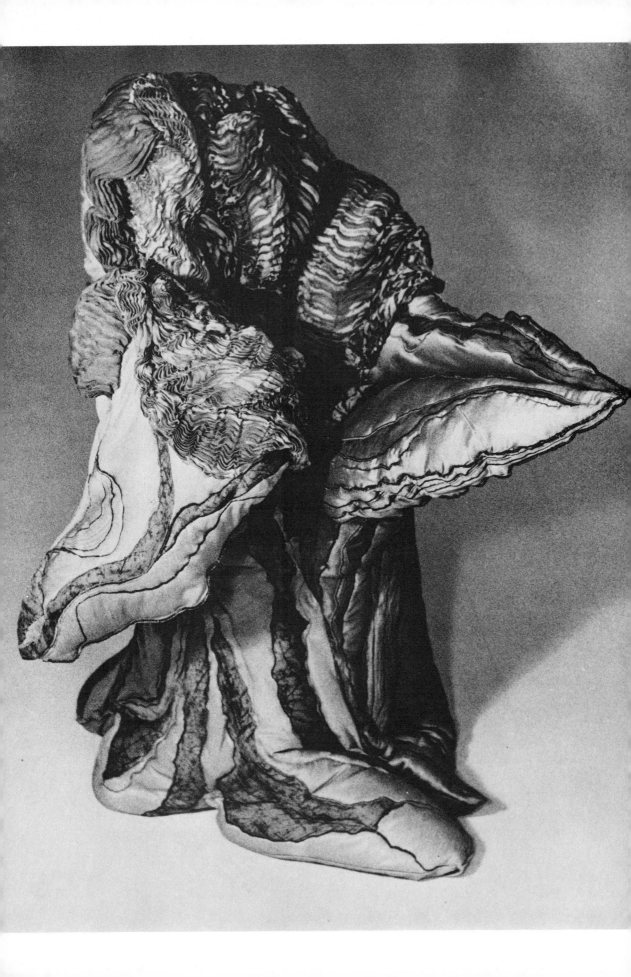

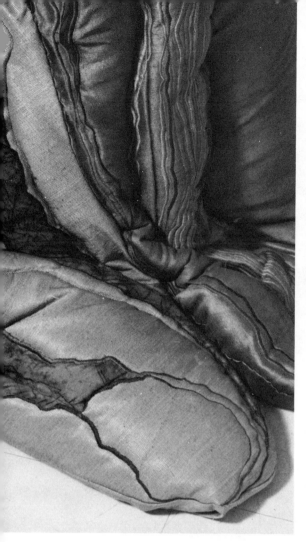

STANDING PIECE

Bernice Colman

Soft sculpture can exhibit all of the richness of color, shape, and detail of any art form, with perhaps unique characteristics of its own. Color, shape, and unusual technique combine to create a most exciting piece in this artist's hands. Without color, shape becomes paramount and the viewer can see the stump of a tree. Its color is so intriguing, however, that a host of associations is uncovered in people's minds. To one viewer, it looked as if you opened an old theater trunk full of period costumes.

The stump has trapunto-quilted areas of a lustrous taffeta hand dyed in shades of rust, mauve, dusty pink, and maroon. For the top interior section, the artist gathered silk chiffon fabric into tiny folds before tie dyeing. Here colors range from rust-red to blue and white in the pleats. The chiffon holds the pleats permanently because the fabric was tied with string, dyed, and then dried with the strings in place. This remarkable piece is about 30″ high.

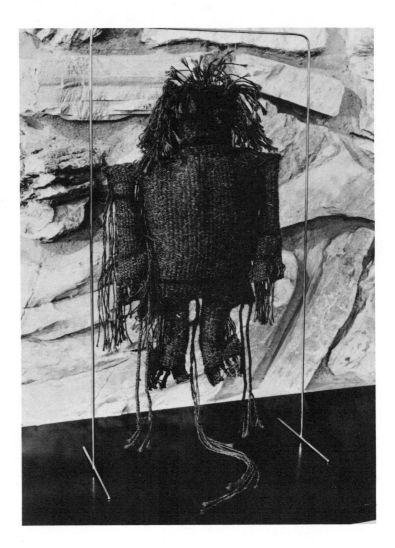

CRY BABY

Michael Miller

Strings of tears flow from the woven eyes of this small primitive figure. Like the rest of a series of Mike Miller's totem people, this one is woven in a continuous double weave that results in a three-dimensional shape that can be stuffed as it is woven. Warp ends are left hanging to serve as hair and embellishment. Miller allows the construction techniques to suggest the form, which gives the primitive flavor. The metal framework provides a consistent and unobtrusive means of displaying the figure as an art object.

Overall height is about 15″. Softly spun wools in dark natural colors maintain the look of antiquity.

EIGHT BALLS

Huruno Iwashiro

Eight elegant balls in richly colored velvet represent also the various fascinating stages of growth of the artist's expected child. Each ball, in graduated sizes, is screen-printed velvet sewn into wedge shapes and assembled into a spherical shape. The final largest ball opens in half to reveal the inside. (See color page.) Each of the globes has a design pattern that relates to and enhances the shape. The sizes range from 6″ to 30″.

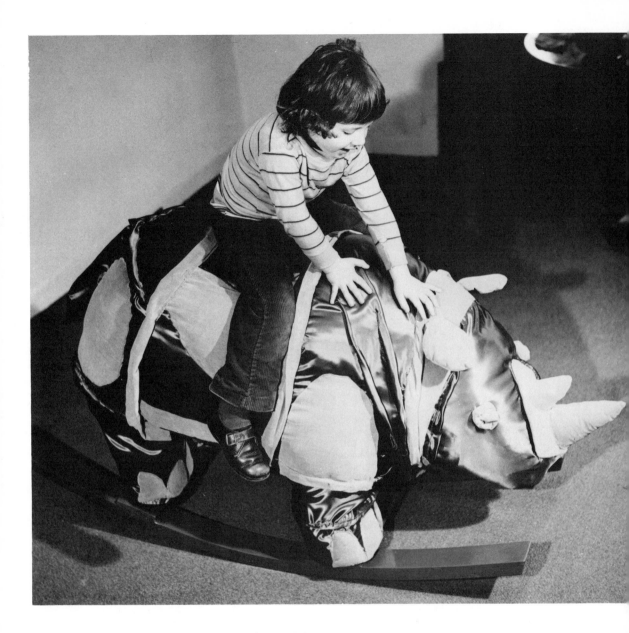

PURPLE RHINOCEROS

Dorothy Zeidman Lipski

"This rhinoceros-rocker was an attempt to resolve two problems: that of using a solid armature and the idea of making a realistic animal. I wanted to test my ideas of fantasy and reality. I like the soft touch of this hard piece and the luxurious satin that emphasizes the softness," says the artist.

Collin Hall, shown test riding the rocking rhino, hinted that he certainly would like to own it. "I think it would fit through our front door, and wouldn't my mother be surprised to find him in our living room!"

4. toys

Toys are for children—small ones and grown-up ones. They offer a world of charm and whimsy to enjoy. I always feel a little sorry for people who think they must always act grown up, construing it to mean they should not delight in simple pleasures.

Antonia Fraser begins her book *A History of Toys* with a marvelous statement: ''The nature of toys is compounded of pleasure, fantasy and imitation. The history of toys is made up of contrasts, and lies somewhere between the need of the child, the interest of the historian, the desire of the collector, and last but not least, the involvement of the adult in his childhood—the magic world, from which he cannot bear to be excluded forever by the mere act of growing up.''

Psychologists feel that toys must be of enormous importance to children since they use them in their free play to work out their fears and concerns. Toys provide a chance for children to experiment in fantasy and reality, to accept limitations, and control real behavior. This describes the maturing process—to pass from the dream world to the real one, a trip still made often long past childhood.

Just as you may, I remember my favorite childhood toy intimately. Little Teddy was not new when I found him, and it may have been this bedraggled state that appealed to me. My mother replaced his missing eyes with buttons. (No future bear could have real glass eyes since he didn't.) Brown crepe fabric petals from an old corsage provided ears. Stretchy patches held his remaining sawdust from leaking. It must have been the texture of his soft huggable shape and the contrast of little remaining patches of golden plush hair with the worn brown fabric of his pelt, that endeared him to me. My last look at old Teddy occurred years later when moths had drained him of all sawdust. As a hopelessly worn-out toy, I tried to view him objectively to see what about him had appealed to me. His funny stitched mouth still smiled at me and his underwear-button eyes knowingly shared all those years of growing.

The powerful grip of the fantasy world has always been a part of human nature. Before its demise, *Life* magazine published an article that showed famous people with their childhood Teddy bears. To see a famous elder statesman judiciously seated, holding his ancient bear was a bit incongruous but nostalgic too. The article represented a valid step forward toward accepting nostalgia as a significant part of life, and allowed many others to admit and cherish their childhood fantasies more freely.

Artists make free use of their fantasies. Psychoanalyst Sigmund Freud described the creative process as dealing with these imaginings. He notes that most people daydream. Who hasn't discovered his thoughts wandering away from a dull scene to make a more interesting one in his mind. Freud determined that artists, painters, musicians, poets, and others use these fantasies to make art. Their skill comes in their special ability to embody their personal fantasies in aesthetic form—a painting, a poem, a song. Others can then share their insights and discoveries.

If all of this makes dealing with a subject as simple and direct as stuffed toys seem complex, it is because of the similarity between stuffed toys and soft sculpture. In form and content they are both very much alike. Stuffed toys and soft sculpture are serious fantasy forms used by people to relate to the real world; at the same time they are whimsical and fun, made for enjoyment.

Stuffed toys appeared in ancient history long before soft sculpture. Most rag dolls are loved to extinction, but one rare example remains from Greek and Roman times. Historians are cautious about describing small dolls and animals found from long ago as toys. Just as often, they are ritual objects whose use was magical or religious. Possibly, as with the American Indians of the Southwest, these ritual dolls were given to the children after the ceremonies to play with and learn the adult rituals.

The distinction between stuffed toys and soft sculpture lies mainly in use. The soft sculpture exists as an object to view and react to. Stuffed toys are for active use and enjoyment.

Techniques and materials used in making these toys are generally the same as those described in the chapters on quilts and soft sculpture. In addition, more hard materials are used: wood, wire, buttons, beads, and others to meet the functional requirement of the toys and furniture.

MODULAR DOLLS

Nancy Church

Do something three-dimensional with a block-print design—that's how the class assignment read. Nancy Church was inspired by the beautiful way in which the Northwest Indians or the Indians of the Southwest handled their design shapes.

The block-print design enlarged provides the shape for these 20" dolls lightly stuffed with polyester. Colors are dark brown and white, which helps maintain the primitive character of the pieces.

CHIPPEWA INDIAN DOLLS

Cranbrook Institute of Science collection

The extraordinary universality of toys impresses historians. Again and again the same basic shape emerges from races who could not possibly have been in touch with each other's cultures.

These Indian-made dolls were given to children for play in the same way mothers through the ages have given their children similar dolls. The dolls furnish a chance for children to act out different roles in preparation for adulthood.

Our American Indian culture reveals an amazing array of sewn objects that cover nearly every need in their lives; clothing, tents, containers for food, religious objects, decorative pieces, and toys, to name a few. The Indians were aesthetic creators and functional designers, as attested to by the current rediscovery and enduring popularity of their works.

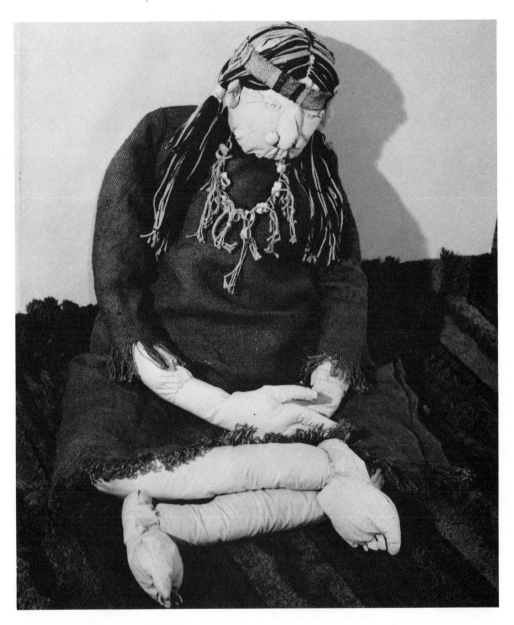

INDIAN DOLL

Brooke Greeson

People can't resist people as subject matter since people can be presented in such a fantastic variety of ways. American Indians are currently popular subject matter with many artists. Brooke Greeson uses burlap to simulate an Indian woman's buckskin dress, bones, and twine to form a necklace, and a handwoven headband to keep her graying hair in place. Soft stuffing keeps the figures seated in an upright position but also allows for a comfortable tired slump. The figure is life size.

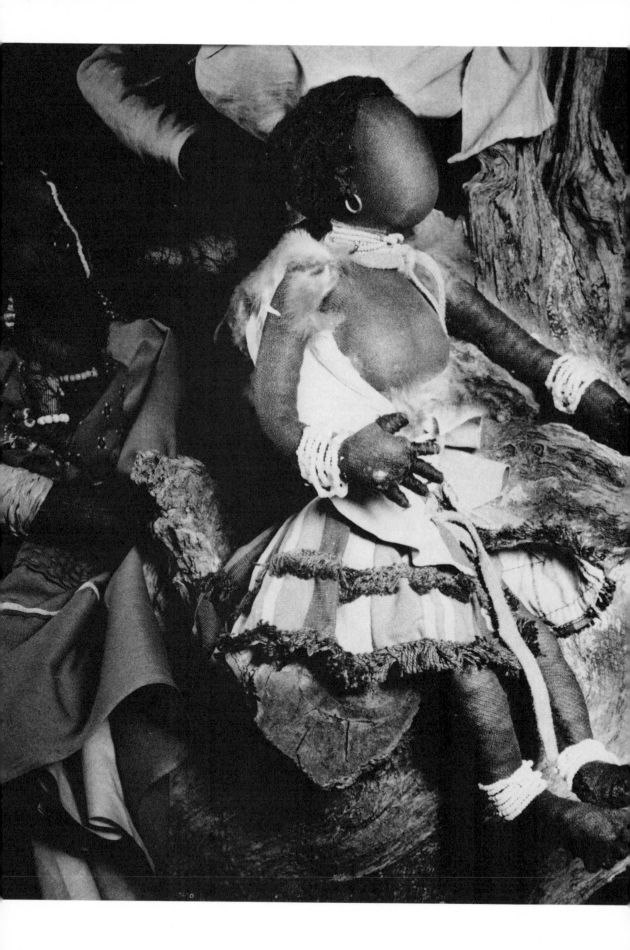

DOLLS

Christine Baker

Soft doll figures can be squeezed into varied positions. Because they have such a lively flexibility and so much gesture in the bodies, this artist doesn't feel the need for facial details. In fact, she avoids them because she doesn't like the fixed expressions of conventional dolls. Christine Baker teaches doll making at Heritage House in Detroit.

Relatives in Africa viewed Christine's dolls with suspicion during her visit there. They were afraid she might be practicing voodoo.

The dolls are made of nylon stockings bound with thread over soft, shaped bodies. These figures are 18″ to 24″ tall.

105

CHILD

Brooke Greeson

Bigger than life size, this doll is part of a family group that includes a mother and a father. A chicken-wire framework makes a lightweight but strong armature to hold her erect. The muslin body is dyed pink, blue, brown, as necessary for different parts of the body. Fabrics were wadded tightly in the dyeing process (to wring out the water) and left unpressed to give additional surface texture.

106

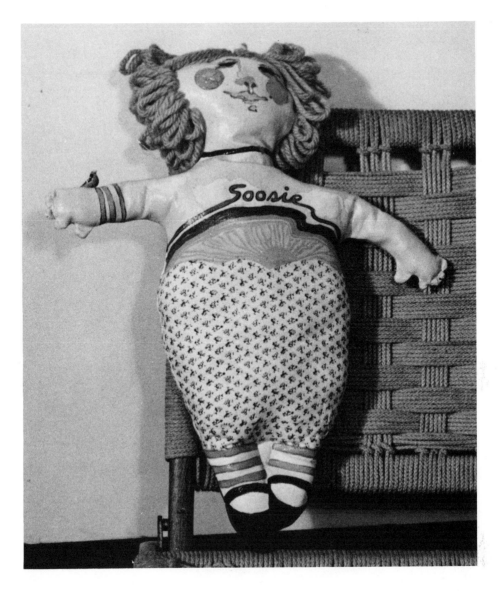

SOOSIE

Mary Towne

This simple stuffed doll relates to the role of her creator Mary Towne, a window display designer. Fashion touches are apparent in the doll's sophisticated face, her painted-on jewelry, and the decorative treatment of the figure.

In contrast to the soft dolls shown, this toy's fabric body was hardened with glue and gesso (slaked plaster and glue used to size painters' canvases) to provide a painting surface. This results in a doll used more for viewing than for playing.

Acrylic paint in pink and green plus other touches of color covers the rose-patterned fabric body. Yarn hair was glued on last.

107

TINY LADY

Marilyn Vickary

This tiny figure—only 6" high—is made of a flour, salt, and water clay that bakes in a normal oven to a strong durable material. High school student Marilyn Vickary began with the tiny photograph shown in the mirror to create a "real" portrait in three dimensions. The body is stuffed and flexible. The lady's arm has been moved aside for photographing, but normally she views herself in the mirror. Choice of materials is consistent in this piece since all are scaled to the tiny size of the lady.

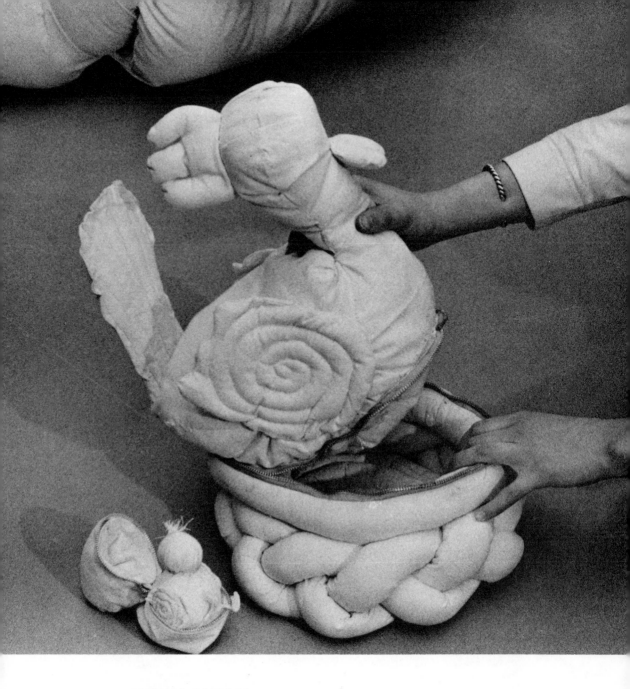

MAMMA MAMMA

Lori Tannenbaum

Zippers allow the baby chick to pop in and out of his egg, and to hide in the nest under his mother too. Although this student-artist has used unbleached muslin only, the shapes and detailing easily convey a warm humor. Muslin is treated almost like clay in this toy scene. Tubes of stuffed fabric are braided to form a most appealing nest. The pair is slightly larger than life size.

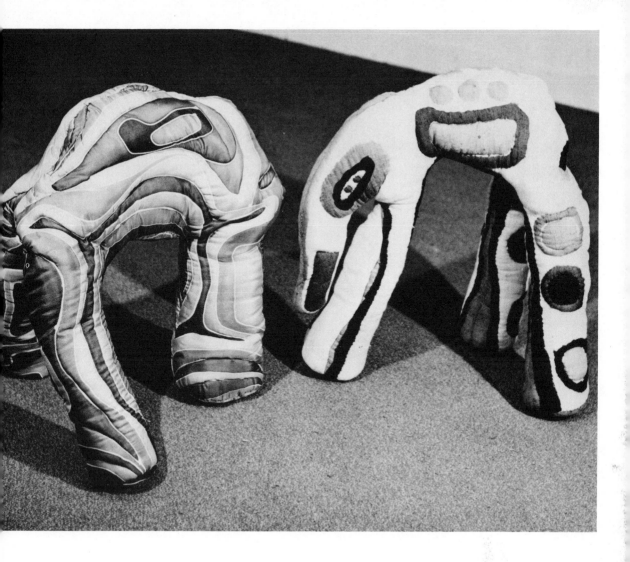

SOFT TOYS

Dorothy Zeidman Lipski

Stuffed toy shapes provide experimental form for graduate student Dotsy Lipski. She says that her concerns over the past school year have been primarily with the idea of utilizing hard and soft in fantasy forms. At first she placed a lot of emphasis on her forms standing upright as the elephant shapes do. They are weighted with rocks. Their body surface is screen printed in colorful patterns and quilted before stuffing. Both are about 24″ high.

Eventually Dotsy began to realize that soft and fuzzy cloth turned into a stiff upright form was a contradiction for her, so she no longer stuffs her animals as tightly as before. Instead she capitalizes on the numerous stances they make by themselves just flopped on the floor. The rabbit held by the small boy is an example. It is done in a miscellany of fabrics and colors.

BIRD BOOK

Brooke Greeson

"Any assignment that I can do in an art form, I do," is this college student's credo. The wings of the stuffed bird contain a lengthy report on flight, which is considerably enlivened by this novel treatment. The bird's body and wings are made of natural white muslin fitted over a wire framework, then softly stuffed. Wire legs wrapped with twine closely resemble real bird legs. The bird book is about 8" high.

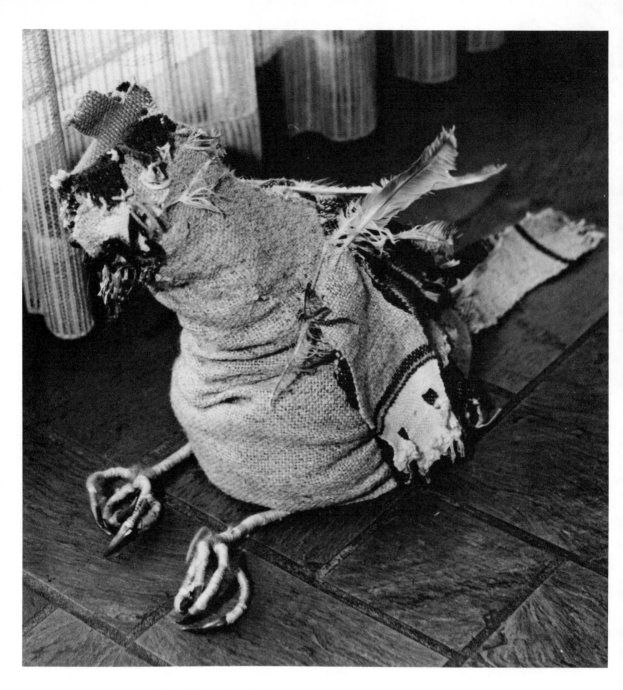

STUFFED CHICKEN

Robin Greeson

This funny lovable chicken is an experiment in shaped weaving. Wings, tail and comb are woven to shape (using the tapestry weave) while on the loom. Linen, wool, and raffia in grays and blacks with a red beak make up the body. Feet are copper claws bound with orange cord. Real chicken feathers complete this larger than life-sized fowl.

114

LLAMA

Robin Greeson

Soft natural leather and sheep's wool make up a delightful llama, the South American animal that provides food, clothing, and transportation for its owner. The suede leather legs and head are hand sewn. Loose sheep's wool is sewn to the body. Beads form his eyes. The playful small animal (12" tall) is stuffed with cotton.

RAM

Michael Miller

A sheep owned as a child prompted construction of this full-sized ram. Soft sculptures often have hard armatures or sections for support. Here a keg is used for the body supported by carved wooden legs. The head is woven and stuffed, with wire added to twirl the horns into shape. Raw wool, which has been washed but not spun, covers his body.

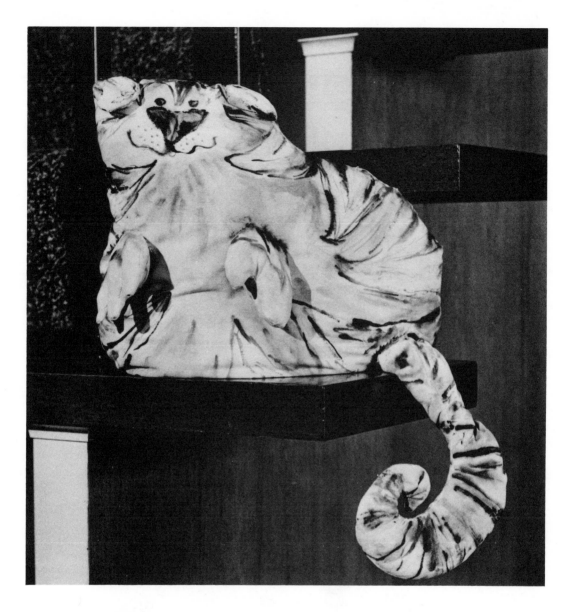

CAT

Robin Greeson

People commonly identify with pets and give them real or projected personalities. Cartoon animals are often given human characteristics so we can laugh at ourselves, and so we can love the animals on our terms. Robin Greeson projects a personality that is readily recognizable with this cat's enlarged nose, loose ripply mouth, and small close-together eyes.

Construction of this toy is simple. A casual pattern of muslin was cut, sewn, and painted with pink, red, orange, and purple acrylic paints on white cotton. The baggie beastie is softly stuffed with polyester. It measures 12×15".

117

PUNCH AND JUDY

Carolyn Hall

The most famous puppet characters of all, Punch and Judy, serve as subjects for this stage scene. Figures and curtains are lightly stuffed and appliquéd onto a black background. Stage lights across the bottom and other details are crewel embroidered. Canvas stretchers provide a frame for holding the background fabric. Building moldings are used to construct the outside frame.

GAME BLANKET

Carolyn Hall

This endless game presented in super scale can be played with stuffed game pieces. Brightly colored wool squares in cobalt blue, yellow, orange, tomato-red, and a variety of other colors are appliquéd on a black wool backing and highlighted with crewel embroidery.

The quilt can be displayed by slipping rods into pockets sewn in the top and bottom. Normally the game blanket is used as a coverlet by owner John McKinney, co-owner of the Birmingham Gallery. The overall size is 5×7'.

ANTIQUE DOLL

Lori Tannenbaum

Psychiatrists have long marveled at the way people "pun" their problems. A problem that is casually referred to as a pain-in-the-neck by someone sometimes becomes a real pain in the neck for that person. Lori Tannenbaum visually reveals the location of her pain caused by moving to another area.

The doll's bleak blank face and body are photographic-screen printed from an original old doll with a jointed body. Four screens were used to print pink, brown, black, and blue in appropriate areas on cotton muslin. Zipper front opening reveals internal organs, sewn, stuffed, and attached inside the body by cords. Doll is 20" high.

GIRL SCOUT, GRANDMA, GANGSTER, AND RITA

Brooke Greeson

Marionettes with movable parts that include flapping tongues are "for fun and to play with." Heads, arms, and legs are made from flour, salt, and water clay, and bodies are of stuffed muslin. A wide variety of other materials are used to create these characters: colored fabrics for clothes, raw wool for hair, rhinestone jewelry, actual Girl Scout pins, pearl beads, leather purse, black nylon stockings, and so on. Brooke and Robin Greeson's father is a dentist—perhaps this accounts for the major emphasis on teeth.

The delightful characters range in height from 12" to 18".

KICKING BOY

Carolyn Hall

Step on the pedal and this life-sized stuffed boy gives you a kick in the shins. He is designed to be a "reactive sculpture": you do something to it, it does something back. Everytime this piece is on display, he gets broken because people looking at him become aggressive. First the viewer steps tentatively to see what happens. The boy's foot and arms jump up in the manner of the ancient pull-the-string toys, and his hard little shoe kicks. The irritated viewer stamps harder on the pedal. The boy kicks harder. After considerable stomping, some part of the soft sculpture's wiring usually gives way. I repair him and await the next combative art appreciator.

Real size-five boy's clothing, a wig, and peach-colored sewn and stuffed velvet shapes cover a wooden framework sawed to boy size.

COWBOY, SUPERMAN, FOOTBALL PLAYER

George Landino

These 9″ figures provide an easy form for creating a series of characters that children (large and small) will identify with. This artist's own large family of children and full daily class of art students at Groves High School in Birmingham, Michigan, give department head Landino insight into the importance of "being somebody" for young people. He uses his drawing skill to sketch three favorite types: he-men football players; old favorite Superman; and cowboys, the last free men in the West. The figures have sketched faces on tiny heads firmly set on supersized bodies that poke fun at stereotypes of who-to-be. They are so serious about themselves, and yet they are quite lovable.

GRANDMOTHER CHAIR

Carolyn Hall

"How cozy it would be to sit on Grandmother Maude's lap and be rocked like she is rocking my children to sleep." That's how I used to feel on visits to my husband's home in Ohio when our children were small. Fortunately, artists have the opportunity with art forms to turn daydreams and wishes into realities. I began with an antique rocker like one of the five in the Hall living room. Grandmother's face is machine and hand sewn of linen firmly stuffed. She has yarn hair and melted plastic pellet glasses over black button eyes. Her body, dressed in blue wool, is a soft pillow. Although I had planned to climb on, pull her arms around me and feel loved, in reality the portrait is too real and I'm too big. We just enjoy her sitting around the house. Occasionally people even speak to her.

IN THE BEGINNING

Kathryn McCardle

Plain and screen-printed cheesecloth, quilted and stuffed, creates a bas-relief wall hanging (4×6′) in brown and white. This handsome quilted hanging won First Award in the "Quilts, Coverlets, Soft Art Objects" exhibition.

5. wall hangings

Stuffed wall hangings are soft pictures, in the same way that three-dimensional stuffed objects are soft sculpture. Both are popular "new" art forms using fibers, fabrics, and soft materials to construct art works.

Stitchery wall hangings were the first soft art form in recent years to make a bid to be accepted in the "fine art" exhibitions that were limited mainly to painting and sculpture. Abstract art looked as handsome in fabric as paint, so a few stitcheries and fabric collages made their way into these shows to pave the way for the acceptance of soft art.

At this time watchers of the art world, and the general public as well, expected realism to return to art after the long period of abstraction. They didn't expect Pop Art and soft sculpture to present the brash glorification of the ordinary in super scale that these trends brought.

Padded wall hangings have made a less boisterous splash in the current art scene than soft sculpture, but are nonetheless effective. They have evolved more slowly and still maintained their close relationship to painting and sculpture.

The earliest stuffed wall hangings appeared as trapunto tapestries in eleventh-century Europe. Then as now these dimensional wall hangings combine pictorial imagery of painting, the bas-relief of sculpture, and the soft, padded, quilting technique of stitchery.

127

In this chapter many of the pieces show pictorial subject matter with traditional techniques for representation that are common to both painting and shaped wall hangings. The influence of many contemporary art movements such as optical art, hard edge, Art Deco, and others can be seen in some pieces also. This is to be expected since all contemporary artists share the cultural climate in which new ideas are quickly disseminated. Because materials are different in stuffed wall hangings, so are the results.

When padded wall hangings are fairly flat, as with layered appliqué pieces, they can be treated as paintings. In these the artist deals with color and the representation of form, as does the painter.

The more the dimension of the stuffed works increases, the more this art form resembles sculpture. Several artists whose work is shown in this chapter mention experimenting with the interplay of light on shaped surfaces to indicate dimension.

If fiber is of major importance in the piece, the artist handles the material in the manner of weaving, with the emphasis on texture and technique to define the image.

The category of stuffed wall hangings is a broad one with a lot of latitude for variation in style, materials, manner of handling the medium, and in concept.

Several advantages of this art form make it an increasingly popular avenue for creativity. Now, as in early nomadic times, wall hangings are flexible, light in weight, and easy to roll into a bundle for transporting. The stuffed wall hanging (page 126) by Kathryn McCardle arrived from California for the "Quilts, Coverlets, Soft Art Objects" exhibition stuffed tightly into a large corrugated cardboard box. We pulled it out and hung it on the wall with only a few pats to shape it. This is a vast improvement over the elaborate crating more fragile art works require.

More important to most people than the place of this art form in the art world is its place in the home. Stuffed wall hangings are ideal to harmonize with any period of furniture since they come in such variety. They can be small enough for the scale of Colonial furniture, or large enough for a huge modern wall. They work well in office buildings also—to provide visual excitement, to muffle sound, or to act as room dividers with modular furniture.

Materials used in stuffed wall hangings contribute variety and richness of color and texture, and yet can be less expensive than paintings or sculpture. It is these materials and the artist's treatment of them consistent with their inherent qualities that make stuffed wall hangings especially appealing.

IN THE BEGINNING (entire piece shown on page 126)

Kathryn McCardle

The least pretentious of materials handled imaginatively create most impressive art works. White cheesecloth, brown screen-printed details, and interior stuffing are modeled into sculptured form in this 4×6′ piece.

Stuffed wall hangings made by the techniques this artist has developed make superb art for interiors. They are soft and well designed, easily moved or packed, and inexpensive compared with a painting this size.

LANDSCAPE QUILT

Kathryn McCardle

Simple, I-wish-I-had-thought-of-that inventions always seem the most impressive. This artist has developed softly stuffed fabric balls to build shaped areas. Some of the quilted puffy hills of this large 5×8′ wall hanging are varicolored plain fabrics. Others use greatly enlarged photo screen-print designs; dye printed on fabric. The center-cut tree trunk fabric is also used to make some of the stuffed balls, which serves to echo and enlarge this design motif. Colors range through the lively landscape of spring in green, blue, yellow, brown, and tones of these hues. See color page.

131

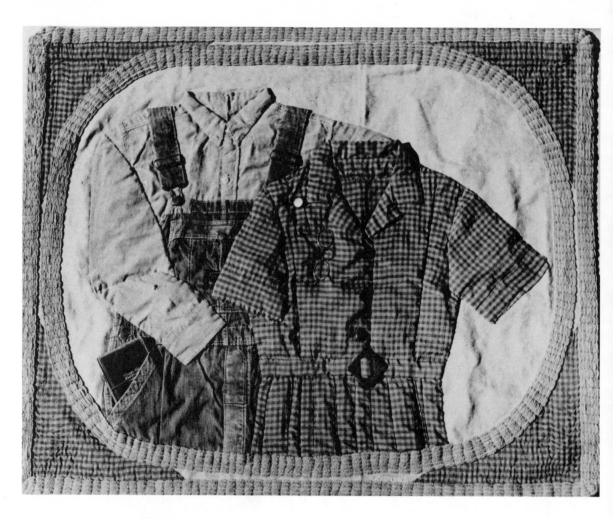

SOUTHEASTERN GOTHIC

Alma Lesch

Well-known stitchery artist Alma Lesch employs actual objects in her fabric collage to create the effect of an old daguerreotype. She uses several devices to appliqué this portrait of a farmer and his wife. He is defined by well-worn overalls (with a small leather book tucked in his pocket) over a faded blue work shirt molded protectively around the dress that defines his wife. She comes through as clearly as he, practical and energetic, and no doubt she spends her evenings mending in a rocking chair wearing her gold rimmed glasses (circa 1900).

Not only are the objects used strong clues to the character of the owners, but other design devices place and date the scene too. Ecru-tan vegetable dyed yarns on the frame, over the same tan-and-brown-checked fabric as her dress, form the characteristic daguerreotype frame. The artist uses the pose of a well-known painting, Grant Wood's "American Gothic," for reference. The double portrait measures 24×39".

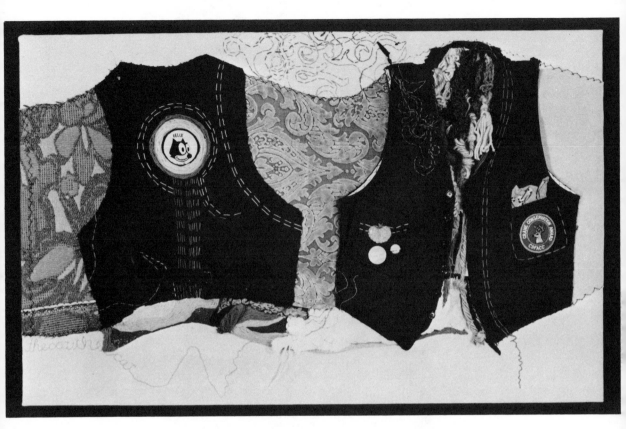

FELIX THE CAT

Marilyn Pappas

Worn clothing carries the aura of the owner. This vest with its rhythmic shape and detailing in buttons, pockets, and insignia is transformed into art. The selection of appropriate plush and jacquard weave fabrics of the same vintage and the stitchery to emphasize and describe areas, project the personality of the wearer of the vest. The background fabric is mounted on a 24×36" panel for display.

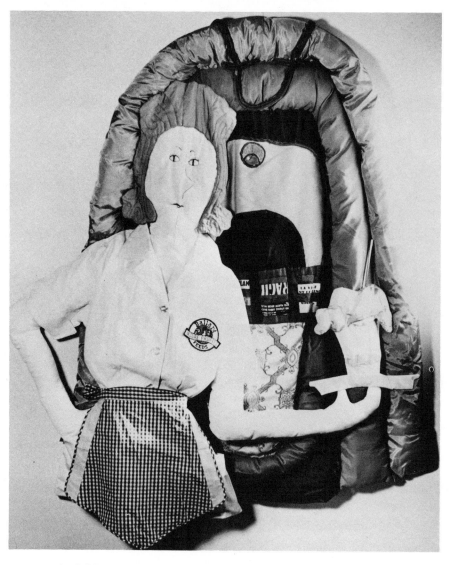

A SODA AND A SONG

Reta Miller

Nostalgic peeks at the past can give a teary eye or a cheerful laugh. Of her sojourns into the past, Reta Miller says, "When I'm working on a piece, I'm traveling in time. I'm remembering restaurants in Idaho, or movies I saw as a kid, the old lady who lived next door, or my grandmother's kitchen. I can't look at things seriously—I see them as cartoons.

"I use primarily cottons, silks, satins, and occasionally a little velvet. Mostly I look for fabrics that have character or suggest a time or place. I use found objects of the 30s or 40s because they give that added dimension."

Fragments of the waitress and the juke box create the whole scene where the crowd meets. Turquoise, purple, pink, and white are the main colors used in this 36×48" sculptured wall hanging.

134

CUPID

Reta Miller

Ancient gods, St. Valentine, sailors' tattoos, and sentimental poetry contribute to our hodgepodge of contemporary culture. These symbols appear funny here since time and change have diluted their original meanings. They are worthy subject matter because traditional symbols gain new meaning by their familiarity.

Cupid is pictured in white and yellow with other color accents. Size is 24×36". Materials are a potpourri of satins, laces, brocades, and other valentine memorabilia.

SELF PORTRAIT

Brooke Greeson

Students are typically concerned with finding out "who they are." First they discover what face they present to others. Then they go within to explore their inner selves and their places in the world. This talented student created her physical self with an aura of her interior self when she was in high school.

Fabrics are handwoven. The face is a ceramic mask, cast from an impression of her own. Hair is realistically presented in untwined rope. Colors stay in the natural fiber and clay range. The sculptured portrait for this wall hanging is life size.

LADY

Janet Montieth

Imaginative ideas can surface anywhere. This soft portrait was discovered in one of the yearly Scholastic Awards exhibitions of high school students' work. Likenesses of people have always been popular subjects in art, since they are an interpretation by another human. In a few societies, these images have been so important that doing them was forbidden in case the artist might develop power over the pictured person.

This young artist uses embroidery effectively. The facial shapes are softly stuffed in some areas, and gathered or folded in others for dimension. You are invited to play the character-reading game by what clues the artists has given. Size of this stuffed appliqué is 18×24″.

137

TRIBUTE TO BUTTONS

Brooke Greeson

Her beloved old cat is remembered in a woven wall hanging made during Brooke's first year at college. Exposed warp threads are tied to a branch for support. Birds and cat are woven in a circular double weave and stuffed during the weaving process. Colors are a natural selection of grays, blacks, whites, and browns in wool yarn. Overall dimensions are 40×40".

Familiarity and affection poured into the weaving allowed viewers to feel these qualities too.

CUBES

Constance Lee Williams

Early quilters knew that flat geometric shapes can imply dimension in perspective. Constance used black squares with added colored pieces of fabric to imply isometric perspective of cubes, and then stuffed these shapes to reinforce the idea.

Since the implied angle at which you would see these cubes changes from top to bottom, there is some confusion. With conflicting designs, where logic is stretched to incredibility, the viewer may see it only as flat patterns.

The piece is about 36" square.

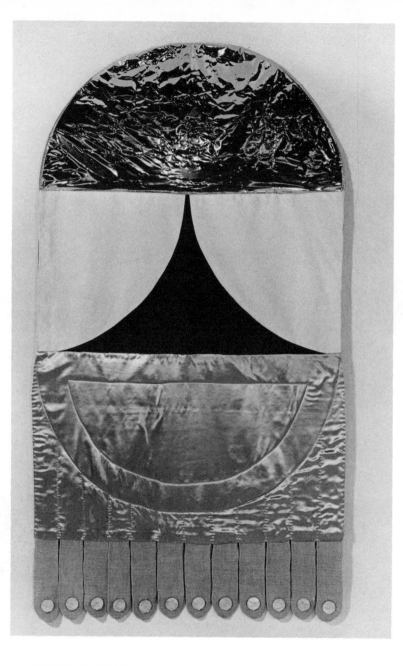

SILVER LINING

Carolyn Hall

Reflective and absorbent surface texture ranging from hard to soft is the central idea in this 40✕80" abstract rain cloud. I avoided my usual color binge to experiment with textures. The small circles at the bottom are round mirrors glued onto a row of natural linen scallops. Furry backed satin lining in gray quilts attractively. Black wool gives tactile contrast as well as value contrast to the white suede cloth quarter circles. Plastic Mylar reflects actively at the top.

QUILTED HANGING

Janet Kuemmerlein

Machine stitching creates a strong and functional line in this appliqué. Straight stitching and the blind hem stitch are used as fluidly as a pencil or brush line. The design takes its form from nature, with flowing diminishing lines and a solid rounded shape. Reflective shiny surfaces contrast with light absorbing velvet and plush areas. Beadwork highlights the center in a change of pace. This work is small, about 15×20″, which in no way diminishes its impact.

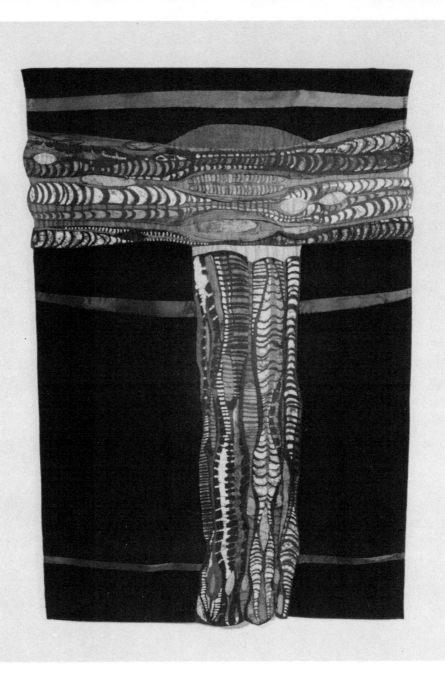

UNTITLED

Gerhardt Knodel

The opaque and translucent qualities of fabrics intrigue Gerhardt Knodel. In this wall hanging, one batik-patterned fabric overlays another patterned translucent fabric—over a third layer of plain colored fabric. Opaque black corduroy surrounding the design isolates the light that comes through the patterned areas, when the piece is lit from the back, to give a stained-glass window effect. Some of the wax from the batik process remains in the sheer fabric to give added transparency. Size is 36×54".

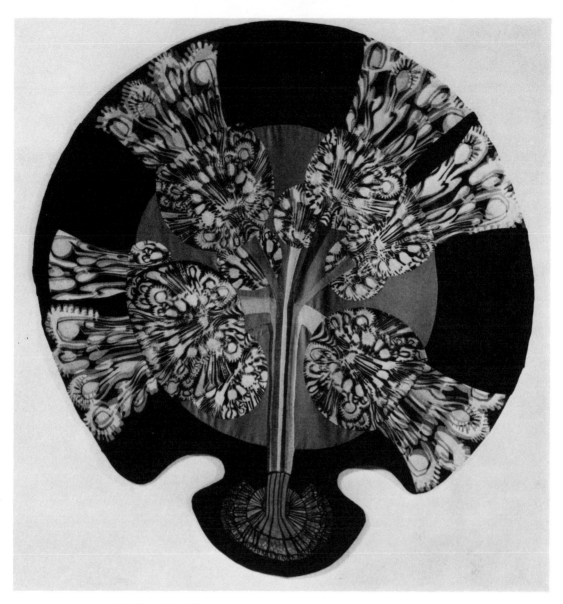

TREE OF LIFE

Gerhardt Knodel

When the light source changes from front to back, the look of this piece changes from an allover balanced pattern to a central tree pattern aglow with color. Two layers of screen-printed translucent fabrics are slightly "shifted" to give a double image. These are appliquéd over a third layer of plain fabric. When lighted from the back, all the hidden colors emerge.

This design also has textural interest achieved with the use of flocking. It is screen printed with adhesive, sprayed or sprinkled with tiny loose fibers called flock, and dried to a stiff velvetlike surface. Colors range from blue and red to the isolating black. The large size, 6×7', requires an internal framework—a long curved metal rod.

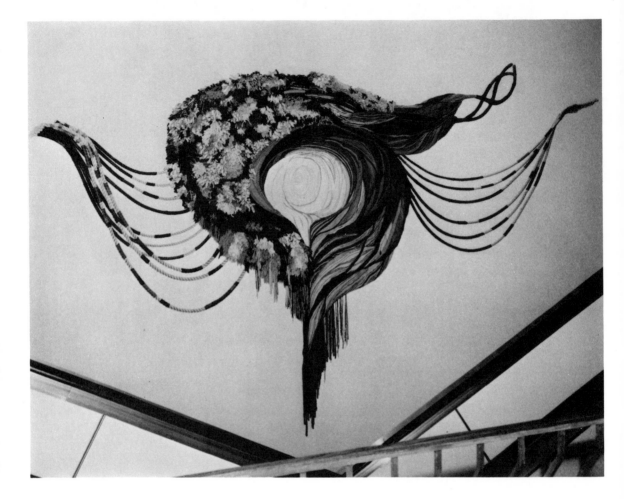

CHRYSALIS

Janet Kuemmerlein

Size is not a limiting factor in fiber and fabric constructions. This huge 12×20' wall hanging was designed for the Alameda Plaza Hotel in Kansas City. The several techniques used give vitality and variety. Particularly worthy of note is the machine couching developed to a high degree by Janet Kuemmerlein to produce the flowing lines on the right. To do this she uses the blind hem stitch on her sewing machine. Knotting, wrapping, and other techniques achieve the artist's desired effects.

ROSSEAU 2

Marilyn Leon

Representation in art means presenting the subject as the eye sees it. Eyes see differently from cameras. Marilyn Leon sorts out what interests her about the country around Rosseau Lake. She sees the repeated square forms, the contrasts of colors and textures, and the random line as opposed to the sharp rock divisions. Still she has not abstracted the scene so much that rock formations aren't clearly seen. Color is muted and mostly natural linen, with threads of olive-green, gold, and brown in machine stitching. Framed size is 24×36".

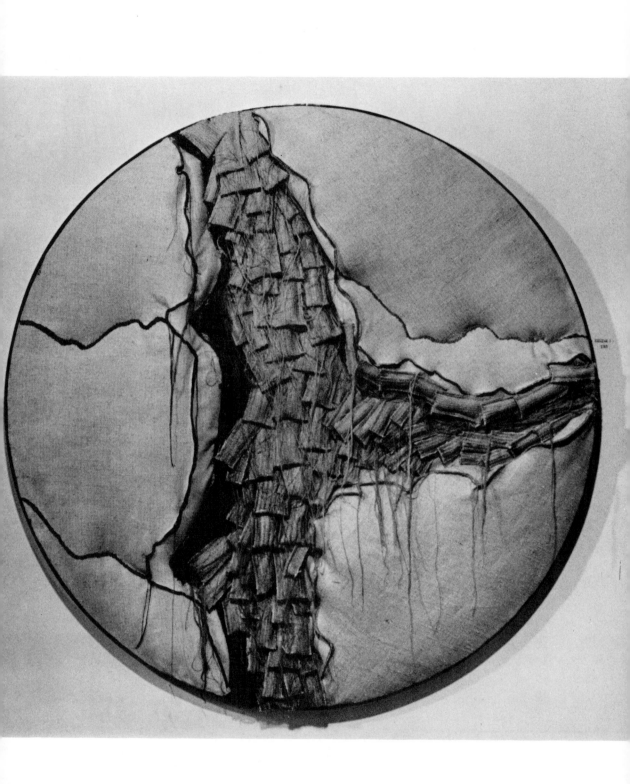

ROSSEAU 3

Marilyn Leon

Artists often work in series so they can try several ways to achieve the effect that best expresses what they feel. In this rock series, subject matter remains the same with variation in the stitch and fabric treatment. The change from a rectangular format to a 42″ circle could imply a look through a microscope or telescope which changes the implied scale. A wooden framework supports the natural linen surface which is detailed with sewn lines of red and orange.

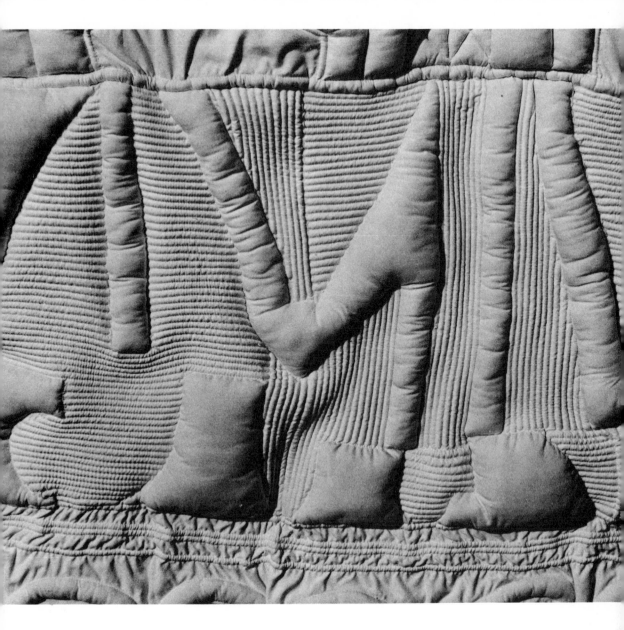

TRAPUNTO WALL HANGING

Joan Lintault

"I am greatly influenced by old quilts and coverlets, so I often use traditional quilt patterns as inspiration. But in this piece I was influenced by a wood carving.

"The idea of all of my pieces is to achieve subtle modeling of stuffed forms accentuated by available light. I always use white, near white, or pale colors because bold color only destroys stuffed forms by eliminating the shadows."

This lovely trapunto piece, 44×81", was chosen as a top award winner in the "Quilts, Coverlets, Soft Art Objects" exhibition.

LA MADRUGADA II

Joan Lintault

Trapunto is the stitcher's method of forming bas-relief sculpture. Joan Lintault quilts these hanging soft reliefs on the sewing machine, then stuffs from the rear to create highly carved surfaces.

The artist's aim, as she describes it, is to portray the passage of time in a stationary wall hanging. "I've tried to show chronology as the viewer walks by the work, or as the light fades or grows stronger and lengthens or shortens the shadows. Or the separate lines can be read as the pages of a book."

The 37×59" padded piece is minimally colored—in white, pale gray, pale yellow, pale pink, and highlighted with silver lamé.

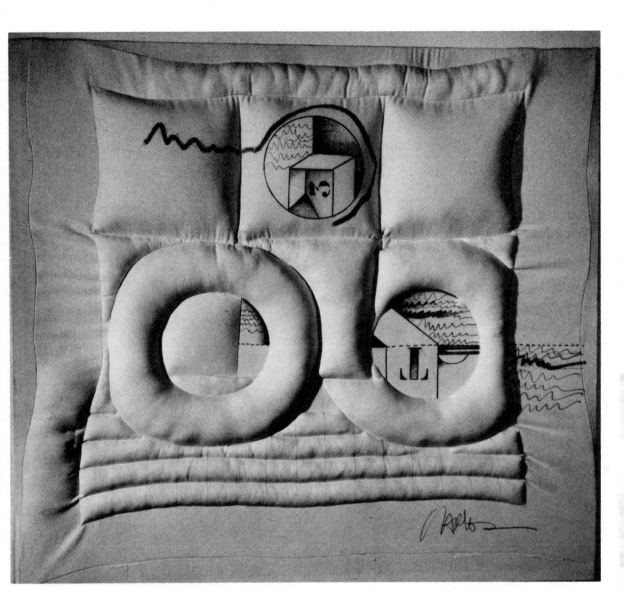

NO. 3

Carolos Cobos

Graphic elements drawn with typical sketching techniques that include perspective and recognizable symbols engage the viewer's intelligence. Immediately his eye tries to make visual sense. But Cobos fools the viewer with mixed perspectives and changing media and scale.

For those who like categories, this could be classed as contemporary surrealism, a mixed-up reality. But an important part of the current art scene is art that cannot be typed easily. This results from the artist's freedom to experiment and the public's willingness to accept what he does.

This soft stuffed painting-relief is about 30" square, done on unbleached muslin, with minimal color accents.

EMERGENCE

Elaine Battles

Optical art plays games with your eyes. In Op Art, artists follow scientific principles knowingly or intuitively to give you peculiar visual effects. For instance, red is an "advancing" color. You see it bigger than it is. Green is "receding," or less demanding to your eyes. Opposites red and green, adjacent to each other, appear to jiggle back and forth wildly. Black and white stripes do this too.

A commercially printed striped fabric gave Elaine Battles opportunity for visual interaction with the viewer. Protruding shapes altered the line patterns, which lead to intended confusion. The stuffed bas-relief is stretched on a wooden framework and is 30×40".

153

CIRCLES AND SQUARES

Carolyn Hall

The decisive geometric shapes of circles and squares impose a strong repeated rhythm on a design. Here they vary in color treatment and dimension. Wool fabrics are stretched and glued over circles, squares, and cutout circles in squares, which gives a low-relief effect. Dark and light, rich and muted colors move your eyes within the frame. This same design was done also in another color range of reds. This one is gold, black, white, moss-green, blue, and purple. The fabric collage is glued to a firm background and framed, size 16×24".

154

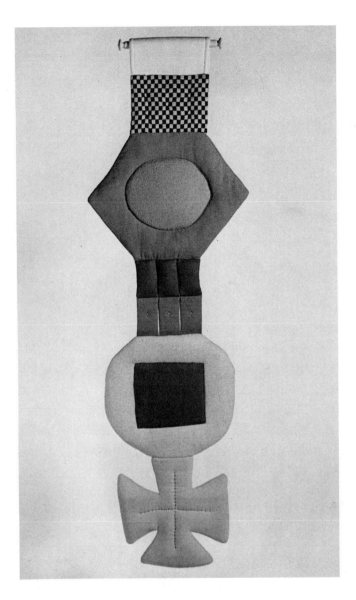

PILLOW THING

Carolyn Hall

Imagery in this piece comes from the shapes, but colors play an important role in the mood. From top to bottom they include: white wool, black-and-white check, rust surrounding orange nubby, purple, blue, yellow tweed around a green square, hot pink. I like to imagine dreaming a different dream on each pillow shape. The smooth stuffed surface of the bottom pieces results from using a lining sheet of foam rubber over the stuffing. The hexagonal piece is a soft wool face stuffed with polyester which shows a lumpier texture. Size is 20×72″.

NUMBER 2

Carolyn Hall

The number "2" was drawn from a cutout wooden "2" found at the lumber yard. Colors range from red, magenta, blue, black, purple, and orange to striped and tweed combinations. Several kinds of machine and hand sewing outline the appliqué numbers. Size is 17×72".

UNTITLED

Robert Murray

Cranbrook Academy of Art student Robert Murray is a painter and he thinks like one. His 7×8' cotton wall hanging is primarily a study in form and color, catching you up in the meaning and feeling of his overall design. Only after you have experienced it for a while, debating if he means the red and green strong geometric shapes to be some kind of stop and go traffic signals, do you see that it also can be a double bedspread with pillow covers.

Sharply contrasting reds and greens are lulled into harmony by darker maroons and greens, mixtures of the brighter colors. The piece is entirely machine sewn including the top stitching which is minimal to allow the fabric to drape and wrinkle naturally.

RAINBOW

Leslie Masters

The shimmering phenomenon of a rainbow appeals to all, and particularly to this artist whose paintings also are rampant with high-key clear colors. The large scale, 15′ high and 4′ wide, contributes to the presence in this stuffed draped hanging. Spectrum colors from yellow through pink and red to purple are in shiny polyester lining fabric. Stuffing, quilting, and wires at the top maintain the shape, allowing fabric to drape in folds and heap in planned disarray at the bottom.

158

6. experimental and environmental design

New ideas and innovative pieces keep coming to light that I want to include in this book. Some are not yet finished, some are not quite stuffed art, and some will probably come in the mail after I've sent off the manuscript. "At some point you just have to stop collecting and start organizing what you have," advised my editor. We agree that there is no end to this field, but rather a burgeoning ground swell of increasing interest in stuffed art.

These last pieces are as much beginning as end. They have the seeds of new directions within them (as do some of the other items included in the book). One major change that has occurred from traditional quilts, pillows, and other stuffed forms to these experimental pieces is the shifting of interest from objects that are stuffed, to stuffing that makes the object. In these art works the inside gains importance over the outside, as for example transparent pieces that expose the interior stuffing.

This idea could be the result of the introspective intellectualizing of conceptual art. The artist's idea is the art, whether it has substance or not. The inside of the art/artist is more important than the exterior.

Or it could as easily spring from the artist's response to the materials used. When people work with different substances the natural qualities of the materials become an experience that brings forth new concepts for form.

New materials, especially the variety and characteristics of plastics, intrigue many of the artists whose works are shown. Technology presents a bonanza of new materials and new techniques for artists to experiment with.

The ways of constructing dimensional soft art objects help shape ideas about art. Old techniques in new materials, new techniques in old materials, and all the other possible variations invite exploration.

In textile instructor Marilyn Leon's "Fabric Forms in Muslin" show at the Detroit Society of Arts and Crafts, all students were required to work with common unbleached muslin to express their ideas. Like unglazed clay, the plain off-white material allowed the shapes and shadows to dominate. We show a series of these works to illustrate that individual style emerges regardless of limitations.

The objects in another soft art show, "FABRICations," indicate that space and size may suggest ideas for form. This exhibition was assembled by Gerhardt Knodel as head of the textile department at Cranbrook Academy of Art. Specifications for the show required each piece to exist within a space 18"×18"×10'. For some artists this requirement was an exciting challenge.

When art becomes large enough to envelop the viewer it can be called "environmental." The people and their enclosed space then become the filling.

Is that stretching definitions a bit far? To stretch definitions, to push possibilities beyond current limitations is the role of innovative artists. Without innovation, art could only repeat existing art. Stuffed art would not have developed, nor other new movements now in the making.

Henri Matisse, one of the most outstanding of the French Modern painters, encouraged those who emulated his works to use his concept, not his style. Personal style in art, as in the way you speak, is individual manifestation of the thoughts behind it. Matisse invited people to share in his artistic and intellectual discoveries, to understand his reasons, and to move on from there to their own personal imagery, rather than use his style of painting with no understanding.

The stuffed art objects collected for this book are assembled with this premise in mind—for you to see how others work in this medium. Sometimes it is possible to see clearly the progression of thoughts and influences that led an artist to an idea. Hopefully, many of these works will lead you to new ideas and new directions.

BAHAMA DEEP

Gerhardt G. Knodel

The idea of this composition is to explore movement of individual elements. The framework of metal rods gives a defined line through which plastic rods move. The soft Ethafoam plastic rods are wrapped with screen-printed China silk and bound with monofilament line to get the spiral effect. The finished piece is 36″ square.

These and works on following two pages were selected from twenty pieces in the "Fabric Forms in Muslin" exhibition by students at the Detroit Society of Arts and Crafts art school. They give an idea of the range of experimentation using one fabric. In all pieces—large or small—the students responded to the nature of the materials. They used a variety of techniques —braiding, folding, gathering, tying, quilting, and stuffing—to make dimensional shapes.

ODE TO MOBY DICK

Kerry McBride

McBride uses trapunto stuffing in his large 36×120″ wall hanging. His shapes swirl and toss to the rhythm of the sea.

FAMILIAL SLITHE

Terry Nagel

Three large identical units sculptured by the trapunto technique are interlaced in the center and held together with hidden stitches. The 36×168″ piece suggests the intertwined relationships in a family, a subject commonly examined by students.

163

STRAWS

Marilyn Gage

By the simple means of folding, this young artist creates an attractive shape. She stitched and stuffed a row of vertical folds. These she crossed with a similar row of horizontal folds to make double folds at the junctures. A large square of uncut fabric is allowed to form a natural pattern by this folding and draping. Size is 40×48″.

FLOWERS

Silvia Vigiletti

Unbleached muslin works can be large or small. Silvia Vigiletti mounted her small 15×18″ stitchery on a rigid backing. Quilted vertical rows represent the flower stems. Gathered circles accentuated with colored wooden beads portray the flower heads.

165

PINK AND WHITE CONSTRUCTION

Kathy McDonnell

Many artists stumble into making soft art works unexpectedly. College student Kathy McDonnell began as a painter making shaped canvases. This influence still remains in this sculptural piece including stuffed sections. Constructions seemed too rigid so she experimented with juxtaposing hard and soft shapes. The rigid areas are white canvas over a wooden framework. Stuffed pillow shapes are dyed, one pink and one green. Size is 48×60×18".

166

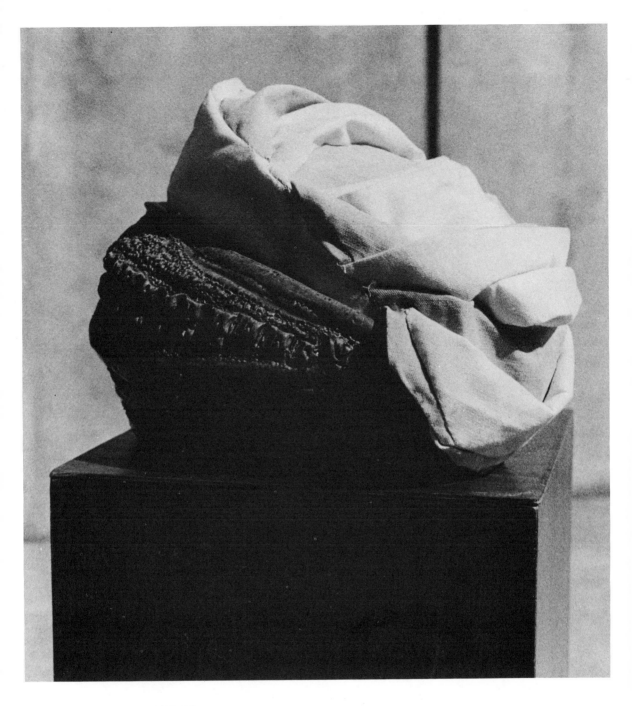

UNTITLED

Kathy McDonnell

Further experimentation developed Kathy's interest in soft constructions. The way clay models so fluidly seemed compatible with the soft folds in fabrics so that she decided to combine the two. This piece of natural linen and brown ceramic measures 12×15".

167

STUFFED BOX

Kenneth Gwi

Soft sculptured fruits and vegetables come spilling out of a hardboard box, cornucopia style. The box is canvas covered and painted a grayed blue-green. The stuffed muslin food is painted in muted colors of gray, blue, and orange directly on the unsized fabric. The 12×12× 28″ piece is owned by Mr. and Mrs. Walter Denison.

NINE BAGS

Carolyn Hall

"Seeing" isn't the only sense we use in experiencing art works. Touch is equally important—especially in stuffed art. Each of these nine bags is filled with different stuffings. The first feels the softest with its filling of polyester. The second has a curious shifting effect with its cargo of light-weight plastic pellets. The third is bouncy from the shredded foam rubber inside. The fourth rustles to entertain the ear as well as the hands when the wadded tissue paper is felt. The fifth is heavy and soft with washed raw sheep's wool (which still smells a bit of sheep). Number Six is fluffy with feathers. Seven rattles and smells fragrantly of its collection of pine cones. Eight is reinforced enough for its load of gravel, and Nine offers a tactile treat with its mink lining. Bags are made of sturdy canvas, closed with nylon cord. Red, blue, and black numbers are stenciled on with a stippling brush. Each bag measures 19×20".

UNTITLED

Robert Goethals

A vast enlargement of straight tabby weaving is produced in full three dimensions by this California artist. Actual size is 36" square by 3" thick. Tubes are made of screen-printed fabrics, stuffed and then woven. This super weaving can be shaped to stand by itself in different ways, laid flat, or even used as a small quilt. Colors are a strong cheerful combination of red, green, and blue with shadings accomplished by incompletely mixed dyes.

UNTITLED

Kris Whitfield

Contrasting textures are encapsulated in clear plastic. Additional variation of texture results from the plastic chain links that snap together to hold the edges shut. The piece is large, 4×6', and heavy—even though visually it appears quite light. Stuffing is shredded newspaper and excelsior.

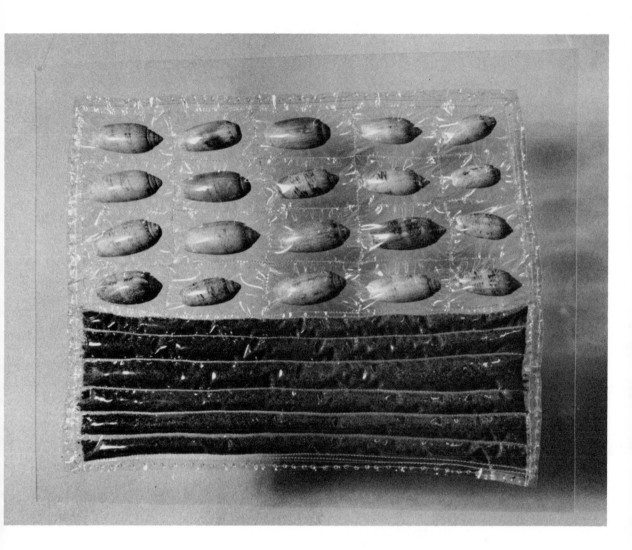

SHELLS AND SAND

Robin Greeson

To find a special shell on the beach and to squeeze the sand through bare toes is a delight that Robin Greeson wanted to preserve. She encased common sea shells and beach sand in small machine-sewn pockets to preserve their importance. This transparent stitchery with bits of nature stuffing is framed by a 9×12″ piece of clear plexiglass.

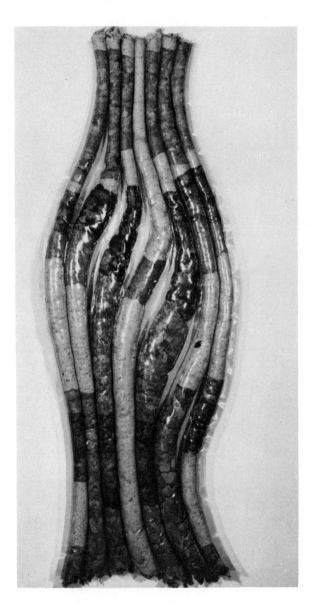

TRANSPARENCY NUMBER 1

Philip Warner

"I am concerned with the honesty of stuffing and with what happens when cotton stuffing is compressed tightly or released from pressure. It's a contemporary response to ikat, the technique of dyeing the warp threads before a piece is woven. This results in colors that are always a bit uneven. I pushed in the stuffing (dyed gray, rose, brown, beige, green, and gold) at different levels to resemble this ikat effect."

The transparent plastic is machine stitched to the backing in channels which are then stuffed with rough cotton. The art work is 5' tall and 30" wide.

TRANSPARENCY NUMBER 2

Philip Warner

"The compressed cotton naturally looks organic, so I used this effect to full advantage. I made the external sewn shapes go with organic compression of the intestinal tract. The clear vinyl allows me to see all of the compression."

Dark green flocking was chosen to contrast with the clear plastic and natural cotton stuffing. The piece is 36×48".

175

JUNE STAR

Rosa Patino

Plastic layered as in quilts is gathered to make space for the stars inside. The top two layers are a blue-tinted plastic (slightly frosted) over a third translucent blue plastic layer. This frosting diffuses the sequin stars mounted on the second and third layers. Within the ¾" depth of the three-layer piece, this college student is able to imply the great distances of the heavens. The 24×30" piece hangs loose and changes with lighting and movement.

176

SMOCKED PLASTIC

Rosa Patino

Old techniques in new materials add up to new ideas. Three layers of rose-tinted transparent plastic sheets are smocked in a regular pattern. Strings that tie the smocking knots hang down to add detail. Each different lighting, each different place from which the piece is viewed gives a different pattern of overlay pinks, knots, and shadows. Layering and smocking are traditional quilting techniques, but their use in this 30″ square is far different.

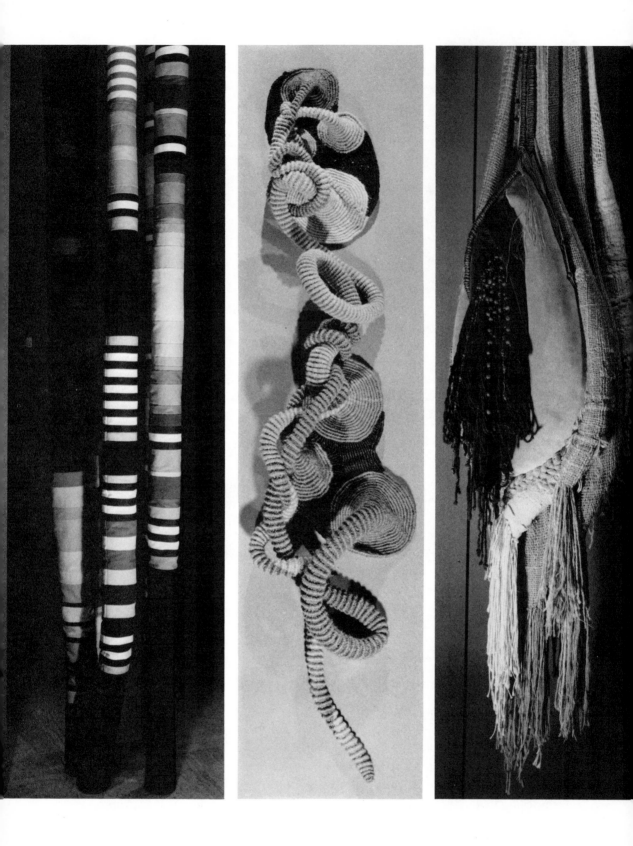

The "FABRICations" exhibition at Cranbrook Academy of Art by Gerhardt Knodel required each invited artist to submit a work that fit in an 18″×18″×10′ space—on the premise that we all must live with spatial limitations. Three of these works show the artists' reactions to working within these limitations.

FIVE FINGER EXERCISE

Richard Proctor

"The five tubular elements were originally hung as a family of columns. However, visitors to my studio derived such joy from playing with and rearranging them that I have decided to treat them as soft toys. They may be worn, cuddled, slept on, hung, draped, braided, knotted, laid end to end, danced with, loved, hated, or, for that matter, ignored."

The tubes measure 4″ in diameter. Mixed fabrics in a bright range of primary colors use black intervals for contrast (page 178, left).

LEVELS OF CONSCIOUSNESS

Joan Michaels Paque

"Fundamentally, fiber artists wishing to work sculpturally have had to rely on four basic procedures to shape and support their structures, namely: (1) armatures, (2) stuffing or padding, (3) stiffening agents, or (4) solid massing of fibers sustaining one another. Wanting to design without any of these, I devised a hollow knotted spiral that can sustain its own weight without assistance. The hand-dyed sisal forms are capable of infinite arrangements within the space limitations" (page 178, center).

SPEAK YOUR TRUTH QUIETLY

Janice Ring

"Limitations exist primarily in our own minds. The space requirements set for this exhibition sounds so small, but in actuality, so much can happen within that space. The work looks more massive that its measurements because I used nested stuffed forms, in contrasting textures.

"If objects are to take up space they must be worthy of being created. And if you liken works of art to people (who also take up space) they must move, have life, project a spiritual quality, and they must emit the desire to be touched and embraced."

Materials used are an assortment of velvets, linen, wool, marine cording, and raku beads. Colors are muted natural beiges and dark brown (page 178, right).

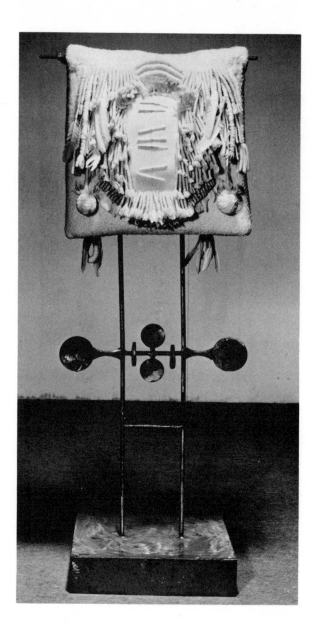

CHIEFTAIN

Jeanne Boardman Knorr

Art objects made for religious ceremonies often convey deep mystical convictions that last beyond their time to ensnare viewers anew. American Indian artifacts provided inspiration for this piece which manages, in an abstract way, to portray a chieftain. Feathers, bound fibers, and other decorations imply the chief's feathered headdress. The bilateral metal stand with bonelike shapes projects the feeling of a sinewy body. Padded wool and velvet make up the pillow shape that tops the steel frame. Size is 5×20×10".

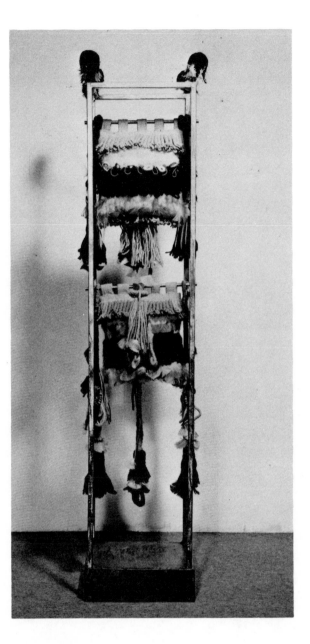

INDIAN TRIBUTE

Jeanne Boardman Knorr

A combination of appropriate materials reveals this artist's engrossment with American Indian culture. Yet her pieces are not dependent on being recognized as related to Indian heritage for their strength. She uses the mood, materials, and mores of the Indians as a point of departure. Fabric, fibers, and feathers contrast with the metal support that is part of the work and frames it as well. Two padded forms are covered with wrapped yarn details in this 12"×24"×6' piece.

181

TOTAL ENVIRONMENT

Urban Jupena

Lush wool in rich colors and a curving series of sculptured stuffed pillow forms fill a room so well that no other furniture is necessary. Rich blue, gold-green, gray, and tones in between gain an added depth of color from the shading of the deep wool rya flossa knots and long wrapped strands. People can sit, lounge, and rearrange themselves at will on this free-form furniture-rug-wall hanging.

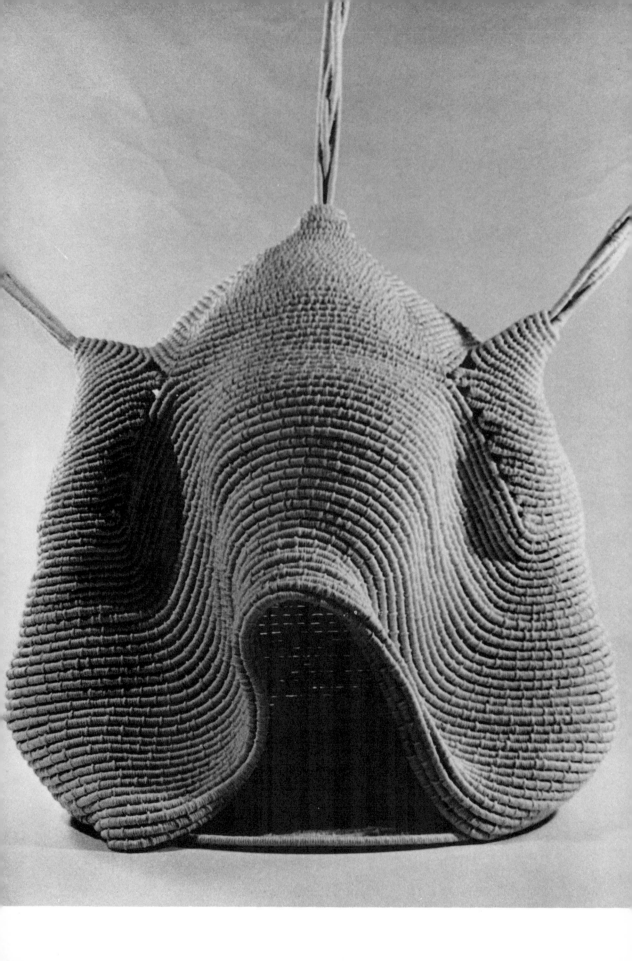

MEDITATION CHAMBER

Susan Aaron Taylor

This artist wove her own meditation chamber of white cotton cording and rope, constructed by coiled basket weaving. It is a collapsible structure supported by three ropes from the ceiling. The interior section is 5' high. As is so often the case in art, the force of this artist's belief in her idea shows in the strength and elegance of the form she has created. Color is a natural white.

AERIAL ACT II

Gerhardt Knodel

A pulsating rhythm that increases from one end to the other implies movement in this 7×7' piece. Ripples of muted colors flow up and down the composition. These fragmented bits of color bound onto the plastic tubing give an impressionistic feeling in the same way that the pointillists applied adjacent dots of colors to add up to a lively effect. The industrial stuffing, Ethafoam, makes a strong elegant material for this series.